# Death in the North Channel

## The loss of the Princess Victoria

### January 1953

*To Dad*
*From Pat,*
*Philip. Cathy Anne*
*Michael xxxx*

## Stephen Cameron

**COLOURPOINT**

**About the Author**

Stephen Cameron, a retired station commander in the Northern Ireland Fire Brigade, was born in Belfast in 1952.

His interest in maritime topics resulted in him becoming co-founder and past chairman of the Ulster Titanic Society. His previous publication, *Titanic: Belfast's Own*, was a best seller in 1998.

The loss of the Princess Victoria has been a long-time interest of Stephen's, resulting in the devotion of four years' intensive research to produce this book.

Stephen is married with two grown-up children and resides in Bangor, Co Down.

© Stephen Cameron
2002

Designed by Colourpoint Books
Printed by The Universities Press (Belfast) Ltd

**ISBN 1 904242 01 4**

**Colourpoint Books**
Unit D5, Ards Business Centre
Jubilee Road
NEWTOWNARDS
County Down
Northern Ireland
BT23 4YH
Tel: 028 9182 0505
Fax: 028 9182 1900
E-mail: info@colourpoint.co.uk
Web-site: www.colourpoint.co.uk

**For Sylvia, Victoria and Richard**

By the same author
*Titanic, Belfast's Own*

All rights reserved. No part of this publication may be reproduced, stored in a retrieval system or transmitted in any form or by any means, electronic, mechanical, photocopying, scanning, recording or otherwise, without the prior written permission of the copyright owners and publisher of this book.

6 5 4 3

**Picture Credits**

Aberdeen University, *Bangor Spectator*, BBC Northern Ireland, *Belfast News Letter*, *Belfast Telegraph*, Board of Governors, Bangor Grammar School, *The Bulletin and Scots Pictorial*, M Campbell collection, *The Community Telegraph*, *County Down Spectator*, B Crawford collection, S Herron collection, *Irish News*, *Irish Times*, *John Bull Magazine*, Larne Borough Council, *Larne Guardian*, *Larne Times*, Lloyd's Register of Shipping, Q Nelson collection, *News Chronicle*, *Newtownards Chronicle*, *Northern Whig*, *Planet News*, Royal Navy, *Sunday Post*, J Thompson collection, Whiteholme Publishers, *Wigtown Free Press*.

Crown copyright material in the Public Record Office of Northern Ireland (PRONI) reproduced by permission of Dr GJ Slater, the Deputy Keeper of Records.

Individual photographs are credited as they appear in the text. Maps on pages 32, 33, 35, 37 and 40 are produced by Malcolm Johnston.

**Cover Pictures**

**Front cover**

The dying moments of the *Princess Victoria*. The women and children in lifeboat number 4 are about to be dashed against the partly submerged hull of the ship. All were lost. In the background are numbers 2 and 6 lifeboats, which survived. The time was 13.50. Ten minutes later the *Princess Victoria* sank. (Norman Whitla).

**Rear cover**

Top: Captain Ferguson and some of the crew of the *Princess Victoria* in 1949 (*Wigtown Free Press*).

Bottom left: The *Sir Samuel Kelly*, the lifeboat based at Donaghadee (*Q Nelson collection*).

Bottom right: Some of the survivors being landed at Donaghadee harbour following their terrible ordeal (*County Down Spectator*).

# Contents

# Foreword

## by Lady Sylvia Hermon MP

The sinking of the *Princess Victoria* off the coast of Northern Ireland in 1953 was the worst shipping disaster in the history of the province. One hundred and thirty-four people perished during that dreadful day of 31 January. Not a single child, nor a single woman survived.

Sir Walter Smiles, the then Member of Parliament for the North Down constituency in Northern Ireland, was amongst the men who lost their lives when the *Princess Victoria* sank. His tragic death caused shock waves far beyond the constituency itself, where the outpouring of grief and sympathy became transformed into massive support for his daughter at the ballot-box during the ensuing by-election. So it was that Patricia Forde was returned unopposed in 1953 as MP for North Down and thus became the first woman ever to be returned to Westminster from any constituency in Northern Ireland. Sadly, however, Patricia stood down at the next general election in 1955, after only two years.

Although we never met I nevertheless feel a strange affinity with Patricia, not just because I was born in 1955 but, much more importantly, because in the general election of 2001 I was returned as the MP for her former constituency. North Down then became the first and, to date, the only constituency from amongst Northern Ireland's 18 to have been represented twice in the House of Commons by a woman.

My connection, therefore, with the *Princess Victoria* is a vicarious one, but one about which I feel most strongly. It is a privilege to have been invited by Stephen Cameron to write the foreword for this excellent piece of research about the *Princess Victoria*. This book will, I firmly believe, stand both as a fine memorial to the 134 who died and as a reminder of the terrible experience endured by the survivors.

Stephen's style is sensitive, not mawkish, thus ensuring that survivors and the many friends and relatives of those who died could read this book and find between its pages a real testimony to the courage of all those who set sail from Stranraer on that fateful morning. His detailed account of the events leading up to, during and after that day brings a fresh understanding of the reasons for the disaster and its consequences. It also brings an intimacy which enables readers to share in the poignant recounting of this terrible tragedy. Its poignancy makes the book unforgettable.

*Lady Sylvia Hermon MP*
*House of Commons*
*London*
*October 2002*

# *Thanks*

To write an account of the last voyage of the *Princess Victoria* is not something that can be undertaken without a lot of help and assistance. I would like to thank the following people for all the support that they gave me while I was researching the story of this ship and her passengers: the survivors and relatives of those lost on the MV *Princess Victoria*, for the invasion of their privacy; Bruce Batten, Head of Factual and Learning, BBC Belfast; Trevor D Boyd for invaluable assistance in interpreting weather data from 1953; Ernie Cromie of the Ulster Aviation Society; Colin Duncan, District Controller, HM Coastguard, Belfast, for never failing to answer my many nautical questions regarding HM Coastguard; Maired Ferguson of the South Eastern Education and Library Board; Stephen Hanson and the staff at Bangor Library; Lady Sylvia Hermon MP for doing me the honour of writing the foreword to this book; Alastair Johnston, Archives Manager and the staff of the Dumfries and Galloway Libraries; Liam Kelly, Wesley Crawford and the Reverend L McAdoo of Larne for opening many doors for me; Jim McFaul for the invaluable help and assistance that he has given me over my period of research; John MacKenzie of Cromarty Firth Diving Services, Scotland; Dr Ann McVeigh, Aileen McClintock and the staff at the Public Record Office of Northern Ireland; Michael Porter of the Scottish Maritime Museum; Ian Wilson, Manager, North Down Heritage Centre, Bangor; the staff at the Belfast Central Library, Newspaper Section; the editors of the following newspapers and periodicals: *Belfast News Letter*; *Belfast Telegraph*; *County Down Spectator*; *Larne Times*; *Larne Guardian*; *Newtownards Chronicle*; *The Spectator*; *Wigtown Free Press*.

Finally, my thanks to Sheila and Norman Johnston and the staff at Colourpoint Books; without them this book would not have been possible.

*Stephen Cameron*
*Bangor*
*October 2002*

Oft times in a home it is the vacant chair that reminds of the passing of friends. Yesterday in Larne it was the empty berth at the harbour that spoke of the tragic loss, bereavement and death. We have lost a ship that had become part of us here in Larne, and we fear we have lost those who had become our friends through their coming and going across the narrow seas.

*Reverend RVA Lynas BA BD*
*Minister, Gardenmore Presbyterian Church, Larne*

# Introduction

Anyone who has ever stood on the shoreline of the east coast of Northern Ireland or south-west coast of Scotland on a fine summer day and gazed out to sea, will see in front of them the swift-flowing waters of the Irish Sea, or as it is also known, the North Channel, that separates Northern Ireland from Scotland.

Those 21 miles are a short journey for the traveller on any of the many vessels that ply their trade of passengers and cargo over that route and it has to be said that on a fine day the crossing can be very relaxing. The reassurance that land is always in sight and that the crossing is short, make the time pass quickly in the safety of the ship. But it was not always such a pleasant crossing; RR Cunningham in his booklet *Portpatrick Through The Ages* tells of a time in the 1600s when the crossing between Scotland and Ireland was not as smooth as it is today:

> Mail and passengers waited until there was sufficient for a boat to make the crossing. The boats used to be flat-bottomed, both open and half decked, guided by peat fires on the shore at night. Horses and other animals were taken on board by first being driven into the sea, and then lifted with the ship's own lifting gear. On completion of the crossing, the animals were thrown overboard and allowed to swim ashore. Upon reaching the beach all persons aboard the vessel jumped into the sea, and dragged the boat up the beach, frequently helped by local people.

Today, at the beginning of this new millennium, there are many ways to cross this short expanse of water. From Belfast there is the P&O Sea Cat, or the Stena Line HSS *Voyager*. A conventional ferry also sails from Belfast to Stranraer. From Larne in County Antrim, P&O operate a fast Jet Liner that can, in calm weather conditions, make the crossing in just over an hour. Conventional ferries also sail from Larne to Stranraer.

Several years ago I was part of an organised one-day visit to north-west England along with a group of colleagues from work. We travelled on a fine morning on the Sea Cat from Belfast to Stranraer. The crossing in the morning took about one and a half hours, during which I was able to enjoy a cup of coffee and a bacon butty, and watch the progress of a red line on an electronic wall chart as we continued on an uneventful and extremely pleasant journey. The return trip that same night had to be cancelled due to bad weather and rough seas in the North Channel and we were transported from the Sea Cat terminal to the Cairnryan terminal, there to board a conventional ferry. After several pints of calming medicine – Guinness – we boarded the ferry at around midnight and patiently waited for the ship to cast off and the journey to commence. About 1.00 am and after some more pints of medicine were taken, the ship set sail up Loch Ryan and into the heavy waves and wind of the notorious stretch of water separating Scotland from Ireland. Before the ship left Loch Ryan, a colleague and I managed to find some free space on the crash mats in the children's play area and there both of us fell asleep. What we missed, instead of the normal two and a half hour voyage, was the ship being pounded by the wind and waves for over five hours, until it safely berthed at Larne after several attempts at docking.

Those memories, even though they are several years old, come rushing back to me today as I spend time researching the voyage of another passenger and car ferry that also tried to make the same trip on its regular schedule nearly fifty years ago.

The *Princess Victoria* set sail from Stranraer on 31 January 1953 into weather that was so severe, that even today it is still referred to as the 'Great Storm'. The wind and waves that day were to pound and smash against that small ferry boat and its crew and passengers. A total of 178 people had their faith and trust in the ship tested and within an hour of sailing the ship was to broadcast her first call for assistance. For nearly five hours the captain and crew strove to navigate safely to land, but nature was to win that day. The ship was to sink to the bottom of the Irish Sea with not one woman or child surviving. Only 44 men were to be rescued and live to tell their terrible tale.

Such was the severity of the weather that Saturday morning in 1953, that today people of a certain age living in Northern Ireland can still clearly recall the effects of the 'Great Storm'. The very mention of the *Princess Victoria* will normally stir people to recall, "I can clearly remember that day and the very high winds." My own mother still tells, to my embarrassment, of how she was pushing me in the pram in Belfast and how the winds were so strong that the pram, including myself, had to be pulled along instead of being pushed. By the time the storm had cleared Great Britain, over 160 people had been killed in England by its fury and damage in excess of £100 million had been caused in Holland.

During my research, which has taken place over the last five years, I have seen documents that have lain undisturbed since 1953 and spoken to many people who clearly remember that day, as well as many people who were on the ship for that terrible and harrowing crossing.

There were several areas in my research that I found disturbing. Many of these related to the Inquiry that was held in 1953 at the Courthouse on the Crumlin Road in Belfast. One area for concern was that although the ship had been fitted with a special guillotine door that was able to be lowered to lock the stern doors in place, the fact was that this door was never used to secure the vulnerable opening stern doors. There was also the mystery of a letter received in 1954 by the then Prime Minister of Northern Ireland Lord Brookeborough, which gave new information that was never disclosed at the Inquiry into the loss of the ship. Another concern focussed on the serious incidents in the past history of the ship, where the stability of the vessel was compromised but which were never fully reported to the management of the ship by her captain or crew.

For example, in November 1951 the ship was caught by a large wave as she tried to enter into Larne harbour stern first. The outcome was that the car deck flooded, resulting in a list developing and the ship being unable to berth at Larne and consequently having to risk a return crossing to Stranraer. There was a similar incident two years earlier, in November 1949, when several full milk tankers overturned on the car deck and an officer opened the tanks to allow the milk to drain away, again causing flooding on the car deck. On both these occasions it took several hours for the spilled liquid to drain from the car deck.

The main reason for the slow drainage of water was due to the design of the scuppers or drainage holes in the side of the ship. These ports, which were situated on the large open car deck, were too small to allow liquids to drain away quickly enough. This was noticed on many occasions and more specifically when, following the 1949 incident, the car deck was flooded with milk after the milk tankers overturned. The *Princess Victoria's* owners, British Railways, chose to ignore what had happened and failed to

do anything to enlarge the size of the scuppers, even though the captain and chief officer of the vessel had expressed their concerns to an assistant manager of the company. The senior crew members felt that the scuppers did not allow water and liquids to flow away quickly enough from the car deck.

It also appears that Lloyd's Register of Shipping in London was unaware of these two occasions when water entered the car deck and caused a serious list. Lloyd's denied ever being aware of these past incidents.

During the Inquiry into the loss of the *Princess Victoria*, the chairman, Resident Magistrate Mr JH Campbell QC, interrupted evidence being given by Mr AL Finlayson, a ships' surveyor for the Ministry of Transport, to ask the expert witness:

> If ever the writing was on the wall, was it not there, then, on that day? The water mixed with milk easily reached the engine room, so what could one expect in a storm supposing large seas, greater than the amount that was spilled, got on deck? Was that not a danger warning?

Finlayson replied, "Yes, I think it was."

While the fate of the ship was fully reported in the local press in Scotland and Northern Ireland, the terrible loss was not felt as strongly in the rest of the United Kingdom. By the time the findings of the Inquiry were published the country was enthralled with the events surrounding the coronation of Queen Elizabeth II, the conquest of Mount Everest and the death of Queen Mary. Locally in Belfast the trial of Iain Hay Gordon for the murder of Patricia Curran had just commenced and within a few days the news of the loss of the ship had already ceased to be headline news. The *Princess Victoria* was also a relatively new design of car ferry that few people had travelled on. The storm of 1953, in passing through England had left several hundred people dead and caused many hundreds of thousands of pounds worth of damage due to flooding, with the result that more attention was given to reporting these facts rather than the loss of life in the Irish Sea.

This then is the true and full story of the day many people in Northern Ireland and Scotland will never forget; the day the MV *Princess Victoria* left Stranraer to become the worst maritime disaster ever to occur in the waters off the United Kingdom.

# The new Princess class

In early 1870 plans were drawn up by the Larne and Stranraer Steam Packet Company to introduce a new class of ferry on to the route, and an order for a paddle steamer was placed with the shipyard of Tod and McGregor to build the vessel. The ship, the first of the Princess class, was named *Louise* in honour of the fourth daughter of Queen Victoria and was launched on 7 May 1872; she first entered service on 27 June in the same year. From that date until 1953 there would be ten ships with the first name Princess engaged on the Larne to Stranraer crossing.

The *Princess Louise* was built with two red and black funnels; she had an iron hull and was 211 feet long with coal boilers to feed steam to the engines that turned the paddles. Her internal arrangements were designed to the highest possible standards, with accommodation for passengers situated at the aft end of the ship. The walls and ceiling of the passenger saloon were heavily panelled and included stained-glass windows. Mr George Campbell was given the honour of being her first captain.

Three years later, the second of this new class was built. The *Princess Beatrice*, also named after another daughter of Queen Victoria, was constructed at Harland and Wolff, Belfast. The *Beatrice* was the one hundredth ship to be built at the Queen's Island yard and was launched by Lady Templeton on 4 November 1875.

These two ships were followed by further 'Princesses', each bearing the names of daughters of Queen Victoria.

In 1889 tenders were drawn up for the building of the third vessel in the Princess class. The order for the new ship went to a firm that was to supply ferries to this route for the next 70 years, William Denny and Brothers of Dumbarton in Scotland. This new ship, costing around £46,000, was again to be a paddle steamer with a steel hull; she would be just over 280 feet in length, have a gross tonnage of 1,000 tons, and accommodation for 1,003 passengers. Her name was to be the *Princess Victoria*.

In addition to passengers, provision was also made for the transportation of horses and cattle. Her passenger

The paddle steamer *Princess Victoria* (1890) arriving at Stranraer. *Aberdeen University*

accommodation was situated amidships and was beautifully furnished. Her captain was to be Mr H McNeill.

Throughout the following years there were to be three other ships, making a total of four to bear the name *Princess Victoria*, that would be engaged on the cross-channel route. All of these ships would be built at the Dumbarton yards of William Denny and Brothers.

The second *Victoria* was launched on 22 February 1912 and commenced service on 29 April in the same year. She was 300 feet in length with a steel hull and was the first of the *Victoria*s to be driven by propellers, having three screws which were powered by three steam turbines. Her passenger compliment in 1912 was 1,426; this figure was reduced in 1913 to 1,081. During her trials she managed to achieve an average speed of 20.4

The *Princess Victoria* (1912).      *Aberdeen University*

knots over three hours. In *The Short Sea Route* the author Fraser G MacHaffie, in recalling *Princess Victoria's* maiden voyage, which took place fourteen days after the loss of the *Titanic*, states:

> Two weeks previously the White Star liner *Titanic* sank on her first voyage, and this cast a gloom over the maiden trip by *Princess Victoria*. One lady refused to board the ship on Monday morning when she learnt that this was to be a maiden voyage.

However, the *Titanic* disaster and the resulting SOLAS (safety of lives at sea) convention did require that additional lifeboats were carried, these being placed on the ship in 1913. The ship's service on the route was temporarily terminated on 11 October 1914 when she was commandeered into service in World War One. The *Princess Victoria* survived this ordeal and on 22 April 1920 she again returned to the route that she had been built for, continuing to give service to the company until September 1933.

In early 1939 it was decided by the London, Midland and Scottish Railway (LMS) – which had acquired the Larne–Stranraer route on taking control of the Portpatrick and Wigtownshire Joint Railway in 1923 – to add a replacement *Princess Victoria*, number three, to that route. As had been the practice in the past, an order was given to the shipyard of William Denny. This new ship was to be built with a car deck large enough to hold 80 cars. It was for this reason that doors had to be fitted at the stern of the ship, a turntable being built into the deck so that vehicles could be driven on, turned on the turntable and then driven off by the stern. The ship was capable of carrying 1,400 passengers. The new *Victoria* was also to be the first to have her boilers diesel powered, and at almost 310 feet in length she was also the largest of the *Victorias* to that date. During her sea trials she averaged a speed of over 19 knots during a six-hour run. Prior to the new ship entering service, modifications and the additions of ramps at the harbours at Larne and Stranraer had to be made to allow motor vehicles to drive on and off. Her first voyage was on 7 July 1939 and her master was Captain James M Ferguson, who would later be in charge of the last ship to bear the name *Princess Victoria*. This *Victoria* saw regular service on the crossing for less than eight weeks, because with the outbreak of World War Two she was pressed into service. The vessel was lost at sea in the Humber estuary on war service on 21 May 1940; 36 lives were lost.

In late 1944 it was decided by the LMS that a replacement for the lost *Princess Victoria* should be tendered for. This new vessel was to be a copy of the 1939 *Victoria*. Tenders were sent out but only two shipbuilding yards replied. The contract for the new vessel was again given to William Denny, at a cost of £313,000.

**LLOYD'S REGISTER**

| 1 Numero d'Ordre. / Numero Officiel. / Signaux | 2 Nom du Navire. *Matériaux, Gréement, etc.* / *Ex-nom, s'il y a lieu.* / Visites Périodiques. Nombres des Ponts. | 3 | 4 Tonnage Officiel. / Total. / Sous le Pont. / Net. | 5 Détails de la Classification. Cote. | 6 | 7 | 7* | 8 Construit. Quand. Navire. — Mach. | 9 Par qui. — Où. | 10 Armateurs. | 11 Dimensions d'après la Douane. Superstructures, &c. / Longueur. / Largeur. / Creux. | 12 Port d'Armement. / Pavillon. |
|---|---|---|---|---|---|---|---|---|---|---|---|---|
| 73435 / 115953 / ~~PDDR~~ *Now "Tahsis No. 3," see No. 95664 in the Supplement* | Princess Victoria ~~Twin Sc~~ / BS* *class withdrawn* 9,32 / 1 Dk & *Promenade dk* *(Now a non-propelled barge)* | | 1384 / 1300 / 1394 | | | | | 1903 | C.S.Swan & Hunter,Ld. Newcastle | Tahsis Co.Ld. | 300·0 | 57·6 | 15·4 | Victoria, B.C. British WB |
| *Foundered* / 73436 / GMZN | Princess Victoria / D.F. E.S.D. Radar / *pt Elec. welded* | TwinSc / ssLiv.–5,52 *OilEng.* / 2Dks / *Cruiser Stern* / *Cargo battens not fitted* | 2694 / 1361 / 1405 | +1 A— Liv *with freeboard* 4,52— *For Irish Channel service* | | og / tt | 4,52 | 1947 / 3mo | Wm Denny &Bros.Ld. Dumbarton | BritishTransport Commission / *Tanks in way of tunnels* 123t | 309·8 48·1 13·0 / 322·8(O.L.) 50·3 FK / B&F284' DTf14'81t FPT21t APT119t | Stranraer British 8BHCem |

Extract from Lloyd's Register of Shipping giving details of the ship. Stamped below the entry is "Foundered in 53".

*Lloyd's Register of Shipping*

The *Princess Victoria* leaving Larne.

*Larne Times*

This new replacement vessel would be the fourth *Princess Victoria*. She was launched on 27 August 1946 and delivered to Stranraer on 8 March 1947. Again, like the previous *Victoria*, the one striking feature on this new ship was to be the open stern which would allow cars, lorries and even a double-decker bus to be driven on and off, making her one of the first of the roll on/roll off or 'RoRo' type of ferries.

The new *Princess Victoria*, with her yard number 1399 and official ship's number of 168901, was of a steel single-hull construction. Her registered dimensions were 309 feet 8 inches in length, her breadth at the main deck was 48 feet and her gross tonnage was 2694.24 tons. The ship was fitted with nine watertight bulkheads extending up to the main deck.

The ship's two propellers were driven directly by two 7-cylinder Sulzer diesel marine engines built by William Denny. The engines had a rated total output of 5,100 brake horsepower at 265 revolutions per minute, and were normally run at a speed of between 230 and 240 rpm. This gave the ship an average speed of 18 knots. Controls for the engines were grouped together at the forward end of the respective engines, which meant that both engines could be handled by one engineer. The average fuel consumption of the *Victoria* for a complete round trip from Stranraer to Larne and back was 3.5 tons, with 2.8 tons of fuel being used at sea and the remaining 0.7 tons consumed in port. Her main diesel tank held 6.4 tons. All electrical services, including deck machinery, lighting, heating and main electrical power were supplied by three diesel-driven 150-kilowatt 220-volt direct-current generators.

The *Princess Victoria* was fitted with bow and stern rudders, which were controlled from the bridge. The bow rudder was generally locked in place and could be released by operating a wheel that was located in the forecastle head. The addition of a bow rudder would allow the ship to dock stern first at harbour. Two bow anchors of the stockless type were also fitted, as well as three magnetic compasses, one situated on top of the wheel house, one on the navigating bridge and one on the aft docking bridge. A Marconi 120-watt radio transmitter, operating on Morse or wireless telegraphy, was also fitted, along with radar.

The most striking feature of the ship was its car deck, fated also to be the vessel's Achilles heel. The car deck was 170 feet long and the full width of the ship. This area was completely open to allow cars and lorries to enter, while a turntable was also fitted at about amidships on the deck to allow vehicles to drive on, be turned around,

The car deck on the *Princess Victoria,* looking towards the stern. To the right is the turntable that would allow cars to be turned around for disembarking.                           *PRONI*

and then drive off the ship. Access to livestock pens on the lower deck was through a walkway from this deck, a staircase running up from the deck to the promenade deck above.

A total of 18 scuppers were fitted on both sides of the car deck. These were holes in the hull at the level of the car deck to allow for drainage of water from the car deck. The scuppers ranged in size from 2½ ins to 3 ins in diameter. Across the stern of the deck were two steel side-hinged doors, each 5 ft 6 ins high, that closed the deck off from the sea. These doors hinged back on each other when open, and when closed they were secured by three steel stays, one at the middle of each door and one at the junction of the two doors. The stern doors could be locked shut by dropping steel bolts into the deck. A person of average height would be able to stand on the car deck and look over the top of the closed doors and see the sea. This type of open construction would not be allowed in modern ferries, which now have a totally sealed car deck.

A vertical steel guillotine or sliding door was added to the ship in 1949. This door, which was 4 ft 3 ins in depth, could be lowered and had the effect of locking across the top of the steel hinged doors. The main purpose of this sliding door was to try and reduce the effect of spray coming over the top of the rear doors. The rear doors were really gates that closed over at the stern to stop anyone falling overboard. Strangely, the space above the doors, even with the sliding guillotine door locked in place over the rear folding doors, was open to the

The *Princess Victoria* docking stern first at Stranraer with the stern doors open.                                       *PRONI*

The *Princess Victoria* docking at Stranraer with a view into the car deck.                                             *PRONI*

elements for a width of 11 feet and length of 33 feet. This open space was originally planned to allow the ship to carry a double-decker bus.

The accommodation for both crew and passengers was placed throughout the five decks.

The lower deck had cabins with berths for 16 stewards, the cook, his assistant, eight seamen, four greasers, two quartermasters, the bosun and ship's carpenter. Also provided on this deck were separate mess rooms for the stewards and crew as well as toilets, stores and a drying room. To the rear of this deck, and separated by a watertight bulkhead, was the engine room and then further aft were the pens for holding sheep, cattle and horses.

The main deck was mostly taken up by the 170 feet of the car deck. At the external rear folding-doors was a cabin for the crewmen who would load the vehicles on board. Also provided were two store rooms with space for stowage of the ship's spare anchor. Forward of the car deck was a space set aside for the emergency bilge pump and emergency generator. The engine room casing reduced the width of the car deck, at approximately amidships. It was possible to gain access into the first class lounge from the car deck via a fireproof steel door. The lounge was laid out with individual settees and chairs arranged around a number of free-standing tables. It also contained a writing table and an imitation fireplace with an electrical fire insert.

Forward of the lounge were 28 sleeping berths. Staircases also gave access to upper and lower decks. Forward of the berths, but separated by a bulkhead, was the cargo hold, while further forward was the crew's galley, the carpenter's shop, the lamp room and the bow steering gear.

The next deck on the ship was the promenade deck. At the rear of this was the mail room, then the third class lounge and bar, along with toilets for third class men and women passengers. The lounge was laid out with fixed wall-seating around tables. The dining rooms for first and third class were also situated on this deck. They were both designed to seat 48 people and were separated by a servery which was supplied from the galley, located on the boat deck above. Forward of the dining rooms was the entrance for first class passengers, first class toilets and the bureau from where the purser operated. This led to the first class smoking room and bar, which was laid out with

The stern of the ship looking into the car deck. The rear gates are open, with vehicles clearly visible.          *PRONI*

A view from the stern poop deck looking down into the open well as a tanker unloads.          *PRONI*

individual tables and seats as well as two writing tables. Also provided was a lounge for the first class women passengers. Forward of the first class area was further accommodation for the crew, with cabins for the chief steward and stewardesses. Passenger accommodation was designated as either first or third class – there was in fact no second class.

The boat deck contained four of the six lifeboats and the buoyant seats which, if needed, could each hold up to 48 people. This deck housed the galley, the life jacket and deckchair locker rooms as well as cabins for the senior officers and engineers. Also provided were six staterooms for use by first class passengers.

Above the boat deck was the navigating bridge deck which, as well as housing the wheel house, had cabins for the radio room and the chart room. The final two lifeboats were held under their davits on this deck; one of the lifeboats was motorised and designated as the captain's boat. At the very rear of this deck, over the open portion of the car deck, was the docking bridge.

To comply with shipping regulations, the *Princess Victoria* had six lifeboats installed, three on each side of the ship; one was 26 feet in length and motor driven with a capacity of 53 people, whilst the other five were also 26 feet in length and could carry a total of 56 people each, making a total provision of 333 places in the lifeboats. Other life-saving equipment carried on the vessel included 30 buoyant seats which would hold 1,440 persons, 12 lifebuoys and 1,566 cork life jackets.

Her single funnel was coloured yellow.

# *Preparations for the voyage*

On the evening of 30 January 1953 the *Princess Victoria* entered Loch Ryan after another regular voyage across the North Channel from Larne. The ship made its way up the loch and, at about ten minutes past nine o'clock, docked bow first alongside her berth at Stranraer.

Dock foreman Joseph Irons had been on duty from about twenty minutes to nine awaiting her arrival. Irons had worked all his life at Stranraer, starting as a dock porter in 1912. He was responsible to Mr Donald McGregor, the Station and Harbour Master, who had held that post for just over a year.

Once the *Princess Victoria* had been tied up, Irons made his way on board to supervise the unloading of her cargo. At around midnight the ship was clear of her cargo and work then started to load up for the return voyage later that same morning. At this time William Pirrie, another dock foreman, came on duty. Both Irons and

Pirrie would be responsible for the loading of the cargo that was to travel on the ship to Larne. Irons worked in the ship while Pirrie worked on the quayside.

As the ship was berthed bow first, loading was undertaken through a sliding door on the port side of the hull that led directly onto the car deck of the ship. The lighter mail and parcels were loaded onto the car deck by means of a wooden chute leading through these doors.

The normal cargo carried was about 70 tons, but for this crossing there was only just over 43 tons. The cargo on this voyage consisted of 110 bags of letter mail, 425 bags of parcel post, 1,000 rail parcels, 2 tons of baggage, 6 boxes of fish, 5 hampers of laundry, 6 drums, 3 bales, 5 cases, 1 parcel, 55 cartons of footwear, 1 skip, 2 trusses of textiles (crates), 14 tea chests full of sundries, 2 boxes of tyre covers, 160 bags of brush blanks and 520 sanitary pipes.

On the car deck of the *Princess Victoria* were 40

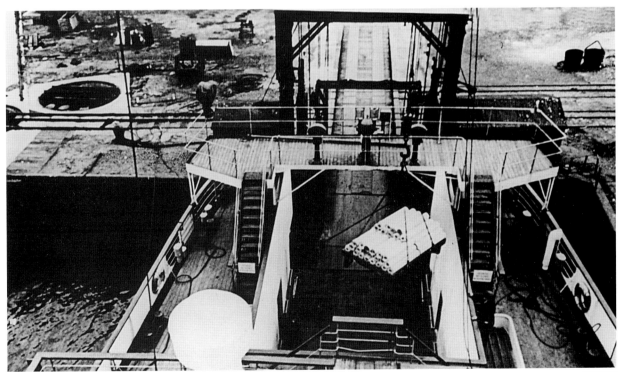

The *Princess Victoria* docked stern first, loading cargo by crane into the open section of the car deck. *PRONI*

Wooden steel-shod tray, used on the car deck to hold cargo during sailings.                                                 *PRONI*

wooden trays for holding the cargo. These trays would be lifted by crane from the quayside and lowered into the car deck and moved around it by a 5-cwt Lister motor tractor. There was also six four-wheel barrows provided on the car deck to help the dockers move the cargo to the appropriate location.

The sanitary pipes were placed on the starboard side of the ship's car deck between the engine room casing and the hull and forward of the turntable, and held in place by cartons of footwear. The remainder of the cargo was then placed on both sides of the car deck. The wooden trays into which the various items were placed were positioned against the side of the ship, ensuring that the scuppers were at all times kept clear. The five laundry hampers and one case of methylated spirits were loaded on the turntable in the centre of the deck.

At four o'clock in the morning Joseph Irons finished his shift and left. Half an hour later, Pirrie stopped for a meal break. Once he had finished, Pirrie tried to organise the loading of some iron bars using the dockside crane. The crane driver had reported for duty earlier in the morning. His first responsibility was to light the coal fire to power the steam crane. Shortly after he had done this, the chimney was ripped from the crane by high winds that were blowing down the loch, making it impossible to use the equipment. There were also two cars to be transported to Larne. With the ship docked bow first to the quay, the rear car doors could not be used, and because of the high winds the crane could not lift the cars into the car deck. One of the cars that was to be transported belonged to passenger James Carlin who was travelling to Northern Ireland on holiday with his wife,

mother-in-law and sister-in-law. They had arrived earlier on the Friday evening, before the loading had started, and had spent the night on the ship in their cabins. Mr Carlin decided to leave his car at Stranraer and continue with his family holiday. He was told that the vehicle would be transported on the next voyage of the ship.

The chief officer of the *Princess Victoria*, Mr Shirley Duckels, went down onto the car deck to check how the loading of the cargo was progressing. While the loading was performed by the dock porters and not the ship's crew, it would fall to Duckels to inspect the cargo to ensure that he was satisfied with the way it was stowed. He asked that tarpaulins be placed over some of the parcels and mail that were being carried and that they be lashed in place to the ship's side. Pirrie supervised the dock porters as they carried out this additional work; at around half past seven in the morning the loading was completed. Before Pirrie left the ship he had the dock porters slide the port door shut and ensure that the bolts sealing it were done up.

Prior to the loading of cargo, many passengers had boarded the ship and after being allocated cabins they had then retired for the night, while the ship was still tied up.

Early in the morning, at around 5.30 am, the overnight boat train from Euston station in London arrived at the dockside. Many passengers stirred themselves from the comfort and warmth of the train to glance out of the carriage windows at what looked like the onset of a very stormy morning.

Ivor James Thomas was one of a group who were on national service. He had just been posted the previous day to HMS *Gannet* based at Eglinton, County Londonderry. He was accompanied by John Yeomans, a 22-year-old electrical artificer, and leading stoker John Stanford who were also travelling to the same navy base. Once the three men had departed from the train they loaded their kit onto a trolley and pushed it over to the ship where it was slid down a chute into the hold. They then made their way on board the ship and down to the warmth and comfort of the third class lounge. As they were walking across the quay to the ship, Thomas described the sight at the harbour: "There was hail, it was very windy with sharp gusts and it was very dark." A few hours earlier Albert Dickie and his pal Robert Deans had arrived at Stranraer harbour on the train from Ayr. Having no berth booked they had made their way to the third class lounge and stretched out on the seats to get a few hours' sleep.

Also boarding the ship were a group of workmen from the Scottish Wig Bay factory of Short Brothers and Harland, aircraft makers. Most of these men had been working at the aircraft factory for at least a fortnight and were looking forward to a welcome break home to loved ones. James Gilmore, an administration manager at the factory, had waited four weeks for this pass. He recalled that he boarded the ship on Friday 30 January, just after she docked, and as he had a berth he was able to get a good night's sleep before sailing time in the morning: "I remember that it was not a very comfortable night, with the ship tugging and straining at its mooring." Other workmen from Shorts arrived at various times prior to sailing. Thomas Curry, a 34-year-old electrician, boarded the ship at 7.00 am on Saturday morning and made his way to the third class dining room where he had breakfast. Slightly earlier, David Megarry, another electrician from Shorts, boarded the ship at 6.50 am and also made his way to the dining room for breakfast. There he met up with fellow work colleagues Thomas Morton, John Murray, Samuel McReynolds, Joseph Hastings, George Sterling and Thomas Curry.

Probably the two most high-profile passengers had also spent the night on the boat train as it journeyed up from London.

Lieutenant Colonel Sir Walter Smiles, Member of Parliament for the North Down constituency, had been at Westminster for the previous week and was due to travel back to Belfast on Friday 30 January when his flight from London to Belfast was cancelled due to the bad weather. A sleeping berth was quickly located for him on the overnight boat train from Euston and it was here that he met with Major J Maynard Sinclair, the Minister of Finance and Deputy Prime Minister of Northern Ireland. Sinclair was also travelling home to Northern Ireland. They both boarded the Stranraer boat train at Euston station on Friday evening and settled down for the overnight journey to the Scottish sea port. When the train arrived at the quay at Stranraer both men made their way to the first class dining room for breakfast. Also making their way to the first class dining room for breakfast were

Frederick Baird, a company director from Greenisland in County Antrim, and Ernest Flack, a production manager from the Pye Works in Larne, both returning home after separate business trips.

In the ship's galley Chief Cook John McKnight had just returned to the ship following his honeymoon. The previous evening he had prepared a special meal for a Burns Night supper. As another day was dawning there would be the usual preparations for the rush of passengers to their respective dining rooms for something to eat.

By around 7.00 am McKnight, with his Assistant Cook Edward Pritchard and pantry boy William McAllister, who was the youngest crew member, were in full swing in the galley. The stewards, under the watchful eyes of the Chief Steward Charles Boreland and the cook, were in the midst of the breakfast rush. Those passengers who had bunks and had been on the ship for some hours were served tea in their cabins by Assistant Steward Charles Thompson.

Chief Officer Duckels was completing his inspection of the cargo on the car deck. Accompanied by cargo man Thomas McQuiston, he checked the sliding steel doors on the hull, through which the cargo had been previously loaded, to ensure they were sealed. The captain, James Ferguson, came down to the car deck where he and Duckels made a final inspection of the cargo and instructed that everything was to be securely lashed down. This task was given to Able Seamen Malcolm McKinnon, John Garrett, John Murdoch and McQuiston, the cargo man.

By now John Wallace and Albert Steele, the night stewards on the ship, were coming to the end of their tour of duty. For the last few hours they had been responsible for attending to the needs of the passengers who had boarded the ship during the evening. Albert Steele recalled that he was approached by a quietly spoken young man in army uniform who told him that he had little or no money and no ticket and that he was wanting to get to his home in Northern Ireland. Steele and Wallace brought the man on board through the doors on the car deck. Steele then went and got him something to eat and let him make his way into the lounge where he was to blend in with the passengers as a stowaway. His name was not recorded on the manifest and nothing more is known about his fate, although my research would indicate that he survived.

Wallace and Steele were approached by the chief steward who informed them that he required one additional steward to stay on the ship for the journey to Larne. The two stewards decided to toss a coin to decide who would travel. The coin was produced; Albert Steele won the toss and was to leave the ship, with John Wallace doing an extra duty.

At about 7.40 am John Beer, a chief petty officer with the Fleet Air Arm who was travelling to Eglinton near Londonderry, had just finished his breakfast and made his way onto the port side of the weather or promenade deck. Beer was joined by nine or ten other passengers who watched as the crew prepared the ship for departure. He later commented: "There was a good gale blowing, the ship was rocking slightly, but conditions did not seem abnormal."

On the bridge the master, James Ferguson, a native of Stranraer, was joined by the chief officer as well as Second Officer Leonard White from Ballygally. Able Seaman Angus Nelson performed the duties of lookout on the bridge starboard wing. The Third Officer, William McInnes, made his way to the forecastle head to join Able Seaman Alec Craig who was stationed there as lookout, while Second Officer White would then make his way aft, to take up his position on the rear docking bridge, prior to sailing up Loch Ryan for another routine trip across the North Channel to Larne.

An aerial view of Stranraer harbour, home port of the *Princess Victoria*.     *Aberdeen University*

# *The approaching storm* 3

While the weather conditions inside Loch Ryan, as described by some of the surviving passengers of the *Princess Victoria*, may have been gusting with strong winds, they were nothing compared to the severe gale that was moving in from the North Atlantic.

The *Princess Victoria* had sailed from Larne to Stranraer during the evening of Friday 30 January, leaving Larne at approximately 6.00 pm. At that time, and still today, the British Broadcasting Corporation broadcast weather and shipping forecasts. In 1953 the BBC Home Service (today's BBC Radio 4) would broadcast these forecasts four times a day. The Light Programme (today's BBC Radio 2) would also issue weather and shipping forecasts throughout the day.

On Friday, 30 January 1953 the BBC Light Programme broadcast the following gale warning issued by the Meteorological Office: "South to Southwest gales veering Northwest later imminent in sea areas Malin, Irish Sea, Shannon, Fastnet and Lundy".

This warning, the first of the impending gale that was to bring so much disruption and death to the United Kingdom, was alerting seafarers to the fact that very bad weather could be expected practically all around the coast of Ireland and into the Irish Sea. The use of the word 'imminent' in this first gale warning indicated that these weather conditions could be expected within the next six hours.

At 6.02 pm on Friday, Portpatrick Radio rebroadcast the BBC gale warnings to all shipping in its area and this would have included the *Princess Victoria*. The radio station at Portpatrick also broadcast further gale warnings to all shipping at 02.55 am on the Saturday morning. Again the *Princess Victoria* would have heard this message as she was tied up at the harbour at Stranraer, in the process of being loaded. Extra moorings had been put in place at Stranraer as a direct result of the gale warnings. In just over an hour the weather forecast was altered to show that the forthcoming gale could be expected over a larger area than was first intimated:

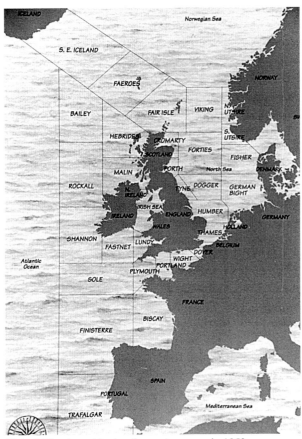
United Kingdom shipping forecast areas as in 1953.

17.55 30/1/53

Gale Warning

Gale warnings are in operation for the sea areas Iceland, Faroes, Fair Isle Bailey, Rockall, Shannon, Fastnet, Hebrides, Malin, Irish Sea and Lundy.

At 6.00 pm, or 18.00 hours, on the evening of 30 January the weather at Portpatrick was recorded as wind south-south-west, force 6, overcast, misty with a squally drizzle and visibility of about three miles. Force 6 would equate to mean wind speeds of 24 knots, with large waves to a height of at least three metres.

The last journey that the *Princess Victoria* made from

Larne to Stranraer would have been through this bad weather, although by the time she entered Loch Ryan for the last time the conditions had moderated slightly, with the wind now from the north-west and reducing to between force 4 to 6. No doubt the bridge officers on this last complete crossing were aware of the severe conditions, but with the weather abating they may have mistakenly believed that the worst was now over.

As the ship was disembarking and loading for the next voyage, further gale warnings were again issued by the BBC. At 06.55 on Saturday, 31 January the following was broadcast:

Gale Warning

Warnings of gales are in operation in all sea areas except Sole, Finisterre and Biscay. Northerly gales will be severe in Faroes, Fair Isle, Hebrides, Malin, Rockall, Bailey, Cromarty and Forth.

Malin, Faroes, Hebrides

Severe North to Northwest gales becoming generally northerly later. Showers with sleet or snow. Mainly good visibility.

Irish Sea, Lundy, Fastnet, Plymouth

West to Northwest winds strong to gale force at first veering generally North to Northwest and increasing to gale or severe gale during the day. Showers. Mainly good visibility.

This information was passed to the *Princess Victoria* prior to her departure, but in the final analysis it is the master of the ship who ultimately makes the decision whether or not his vessel sails.

James Ferguson was long established on the Larne–Stranraer route. He had been a captain from 1936 when he first took charge of the *Princess Margaret*. He would have been well aware of the difficulties that could be experienced in a north-west gale. As Captain Samuel Iles, an ex-master of the *Princess Margaret*, which also sailed on the same route, later told the Inquiry which took place in Belfast:

A North Westerly gale is the most difficult for entering and leaving Loch Ryan, this type of weather seems to set up a confused sea round the entrance to the Loch and it extends just a little beyond Corsewall, a mile or two. There is no shelter with a North Westerly gale.

The seabed slopes upwards between Corsewall Point and Milleur Buoy and can create a backlash and a confused sea. The seabed off Corsewall drops from 2 fathoms to 15, 20, 30 and then down to 80, this also contributes to a confused sea.

Elsewhere on the morning of this sailing day, the gale was starting to unleash the fury that had built up as it relentlessly progressed across the Atlantic Ocean, approaching the west coast of Scotland. The 7,000-ton cargo vessel *Clan Macquarrie* had been washed broadside onto rocks in the high winds at Borve, on the western shores of the island of Lewis. A fishing vessel, the *Michael Griffith*, with 14 of a crew was in distress seven to nine miles south of Barra Head, at the southern end of the Hebrides. Also in danger of sinking were three other fishing vessels that were in the Moray Firth.

By the time the gale was finally spent, over 300 people would be dead in the United Kingdom, 21,000 people would be made homeless and over 200,000 acres of land would be devastated. On the continent, in excess of 1,800 people would lose their lives due to the effects of the storm and the very high winds and tides that it generated. The Meteorological Office would record wind speeds in certain parts of the country in excess of 119 miles per hour.

At the centre of the storm the low atmospheric pressure of 976 millibars, was to cause sea levels to rise by as much as half a metre and produce storm waves over six metres in height. Parts of the United Kingdom would record the highest tides since 1911, an occurrence that is normally expected to happen only once every thousand years.

Across the Irish Sea in Belfast Lough on that Saturday morning the motor vessel *Lairdsmoor*, loaded with general cargo and cattle, had dropped anchor for shelter after encountering hurricane force 11 weather conditions at around 6.00 am off the Irish coast. She was joined by the trawler *Eastcoates* which also encountered the same gale force conditions when she tried to proceed past the Mull of Galloway in Scotland. Her captain headed for the safety and shelter of Belfast Lough, and these ships were then prepared to wait and sit out the current bad weather.

By the morning of 31 January the weather conditions of the previous evening were starting to get worse. At Portpatrick Coastguard station the weather record shows that by 1.00 am the wind had increased to force 7 to 8 and by 5.00 am there were now squally showers of hail with a north-north-west gale force 8 to 12, with visibility of about four to five miles. This would have given winds of upwards of 68 knots, with waves of 13.5 metres or approximately 44 feet in height. The *Marine Observer's Handbook* (Met Office, 1950) gives the following description of a force 10 sea :

> Very high waves with long overhanging crest. The resulting foam in great patches is blown in dense white streaks along the direction of the wind . . . the surface of the sea takes a white appearance. The rolling of the sea becomes heavy and shocklike. Visibility affected.

The Royal Air Force base at West Freugh, four to five miles south of Stranraer, was at 7.00 am recording wind speeds gusting to 70 knots and in Belfast Lough at Helen's Bay, a sheltered location near Bangor, winds of force 7 to 9 with gusting to 70 knots were also being recorded.

At sea the *Michael Griffith* was lost, along with other ships including the *Sheldon*, a trawler from Grimsby; the *Catherina Duyvis*, a Yewvalley tramp steamer; the *Salland*, a cargo vessel from Delfzyl; the *Guava*, a trawler from Lowestoft; the *Leopold Nera* from Zeebrugge; and a Swedish steamer, the *Aspro*.

In Stranraer harbour, at the quayside, Captain Ferguson was well aware of the weather and shipping forecast issued by the BBC at 06.55. Portpatrick Radio had rebroadcast the BBC weather warning and these would have been received by the radio operator on the ship and passed to the bridge. As master of the vessel, Ferguson would have had his officers check the condition of the ship, while, as noted, he personally went down to the car deck prior to sailing and gave instructions that the cargo be tied down. He then returned to the bridge and made the final and fateful decision to set sail up Loch Ryan into the gale that was venting its fury on the North Channel, the narrow stretch of water between Scotland and Ireland.

Even today, with the advent of new completely sealed high-speed ships, roll on/roll off ferries and catamarans designed especially for cross-channel routes, the captain still has the ultimate decision as to whether the vessel will or will not sail, but generally these vessels will not set sail if weather conditions are worse than force 9. Yet in 1953 the captain of the *Princess Victoria*, with her open stern only protected by the five-feet-high rear gates, was prepared to sail with his precious cargo of passengers into the face of a force 8 to 12 gale.

Adverse weather conditions in Belfast Lough.

*Author's collection*

# The Final Voyage

Dock foreman William Pirrie had been on duty since midnight, just a few hours after the ship had docked at Stranraer. Throughout the night he supervised the loading of the cargo onto the ship. He was still at the harbour at Stranraer at 07.45 when the *Princess Victoria* started her last journey. He stated later:

> . . . six men had been sent down with tarpaulins to cover the post and parcel post, this was the 1st request of this nature ever on the Princess Victoria. I saw the ship leave the harbour, the weather was very stormy, spray was breaking over the deck doors.

Ernest Flack, the company director from Larne, was in the dining room having breakfast. As the ship sailed he remembered that it was stormy and the wind was blowing strongly, the loch was very rough and the ship was going very slowly.

John Beer, the chief petty officer who was travelling to the Royal Naval Air station at Eglinton, County Londonderry, recalled:

> The Ship's Officer directed the Wren Prentice to the Saloon. Chief Petty Officer Shankland and I went to the third class Dining Saloon and had breakfast.

> There was a good gale blowing, the ship was rocking slightly, conditions did not seem abnormal.

> After breakfast I stood on the weather deck port side with about 8–10 people, mainly service men and watched the crew complete loading until she left. There was no difficulty in holding on. It was remarked that it was too strong a wind to load the motor cars.

> The ship moved away from the quay astern and carried on until clear of the quay, she then turned and proceeded up the Loch.

> After she turned we went to the after end of the weather deck and stood overlooking the stern. We stood there for about an hour. The sea was quite rough, we were going into the wind.

At 08.06 Radio Operator David Broadfoot, from his radio room just aft of the bridge, sent the first message, in Morse code, of this new voyage of the *Princess Victoria* to Portpatrick Radio: "*Princess Victoria* to GPK – I am now leaving Stranraer bound Larne." The *Princess Victoria* was under way.

As the ship set course for Corsewall Point and Milleur Buoy at the entrance to Loch Ryan, the passengers and crew settled in for what they perceived would be a rough crossing. The journey time to the entrance of Loch Ryan was normally about 30 minutes, but on this occasion, with the high wind, bad weather and the reduced speed of the ship, it would take well over an hour to travel the distance of just over nine miles. The passengers, though encountering a rough passage up the loch to the Irish Sea, would have taken some consolation from the closeness of the Scottish coast. At its narrowest point, Loch Ryan is only about one and a half miles wide and even with visibility affected, the green fields and houses on either side of the loch would have been a reassuring sight to those on board.

Within 20 minutes the ship was passing the ex-RAF station at Wig Bay, about half way up the loch, where the Short Brothers and Harland aircraft factory was based. Robert Baillie made comment to his fellow Shorts' workers about a sea plane that was moored at the factory, saying something along the lines that the aeroplane was still on an even keel.

At about 08.50 the *Princess Victoria* was slowly navigating towards the open Irish Sea; George Sutherland, the principal lighthouse keeper at Corsewall Point Lighthouse, was extinguishing the light in the lighthouse prior to starting his usual one and a half mile walk to Barnhills Farm. As he walked along towards the farm through the bad weather he watched the *Princess Victoria* proceeding towards the sea. He estimated then that the storm was at least force 9, with the wind coming from the north by west. He would shortly take a weather reading for onward transmission to the RAF at West Freugh, recording a wind speed that was gusting in excess of 40 knots.

Not many people would be venturing out in the

Captain Ferguson (sixth from the right) and some of the crew of the *Princess Victoria,* a photograph taken in 1949.

*Wigtown Free Press*

elements on a day as bad as this but Robert McDowell, a shepherd, had to go about his normal duty of tending the livestock on two farms adjacent to Corsewall Lighthouse. About the same time as lighthouse keeper Sutherland was making his way back to the shelter of the nearby farm, McDowell was walking on the east side of the lighthouse after feeding some cattle and noticed the *Princess Victoria* on her usual course that would take her past the lighthouse. To McDowell the day was extremely windy, with the wind coming from the north-west – one of the roughest days he had experienced that winter.

The *Princess Victoria* by this time was making steady but slow progress on her voyage. In the galley on the bridge deck Chief Cook John McKnight had seen the breakfast rush of orders completed; he was joined shortly before 09.00 by Assistant Steward Charles Thompson and pantry boy William McAllister. The three agreed that it would be impossible to serve any more food to the passengers due to the rocking of the ship.

Meanwhile James Wallace, a steeplejack from Carrickfergus, had met up on the ship with John Ross, an

old pal from many years previous. They had both breakfasted early in the morning before the ship sailed. By now the pair were no doubt swapping many stories of past times and eventually they made their way to the boat deck. Due to the movement of the ship, Ross began to feel the effects of seasickness and rather quickly made his way to the toilets. Wallace stayed on deck as the ship progressed further towards the open sea, even though he later said "it was blowing hard".

Below in the lounges the passengers were preparing themselves for one of those crossings of the Irish Sea that would be talked about for some time to come. These included Chief Petty Officer Leslie Childs with his wife Joyce and their three-year-old son Stephen; Wren Miss Violet Dingle and her companions from the services; and Mrs Iris Mooney from Belfast and her two children, John aged five years and Kevin aged two years. All tried to get themselves as comfortable as possible.

By now, it was almost 09.00 and the *Princess Victoria* was approaching the first major hazard of her voyage. As the ship approached the entrance to the Irish Sea the full fury of the Atlantic gale was to be encountered. The weather conditions that were by now gripping the North Channel had been growing in ferocity and by the time the vessel began to emerge from Loch Ryan into the Irish Sea, Portpatrick Coastguard had recorded the storm as coming from the north-north-west with a strength of between force 9 to 12. The waves would have been well over 45 feet, the wind gusting up to 60 knots, with visibility down to a maximum of two miles. The effect of this deep depression would cause the waves to be short and steep and, with the strong tide race of up to 4 knots through the channel, this would have created a most uninviting sea for any vessel to attempt to sail in.

Slowly the *Princess Victoria* emerged from Loch Ryan into this maelstrom. The normal course when sailing towards Larne would be to turn at Milleur Point and steer in an westerly direction. On this morning Captain Ferguson wisely decided to continue on a more northerly course and so hold the bow of the ship into the weather. Exactly what happened to the ship over the next 15 to 20 minutes is still, after the passage of 50 years, unclear. The evidence from surviving passengers, crew, and other eye witnesses is at times confusing and conflicting.

It would seem that after a short period of time the ship tried to head on its usual course for Larne. Malcolm McKinnon, an able seaman, was on the boat deck at the galley door and stated: "We turned around the lower buoy for our course to Larne, the seas seemed mountainous. When the buoy was on our port quarter the ship shipped a heavy sea over the starboard quarter and stern." Thomas McQuiston, the cargoman who was on the car deck, also

Corsewall Point and Lighthouse at the mouth of Loch Ryan.
*Author's collection*

said that the ship was hit by the sea on the starboard side. Perhaps the most graphic description of what was happening was given by George Sutherland, the lighthouse keeper, and Robert McDowell, the shepherd, both of whom were standing near Corsewall Point and had a clear view of the ship. Sutherland stated:

I first saw her heading in the direction of Larne, the wind and the sea were about a beam and the ship was making heavy weather. The time was between 8.50–09.00. Soon after I sighted her she commenced to turn to the N or NE and as she came round her bow lifted. She appeared to be hit by a heavy sea on the starboard side. Her bow lifted high in the air, she disappeared into the haze heading east.

I got the impression that she was turning round possibly to re-enter the Loch. I do not know what speed she was doing. The weather continued to get worse. When she was out of sight she seemed to be on a line between Corsewall Point and just north of Ballintrae and appeared to be upright. I did not see the vessel again. I had the impression that the ship was trying to come round into the wind.

McDowell recalled:

The ship seemed to be on her usual course heading past Corsewall Lighthouse.

When the ship turned it was about 2 miles away from where I was standing. She did not seem to be in difficulties, she had no list as far as I could see.

When the ship turned she took three heavy rolls and when she had finished the third roll she was heading towards Ailsa Craig.

Almost immediately afterwards she swung back to the left into the wind. She did not swing back as far as her original course.

On heading into the wind she seemed for a few seconds to stand up on end and I saw her level down and her screws come out of the water. After that the ship seemed to continue to head into the wind and proceed very slowly.

What appears to have happened is that the captain, seeing for himself the full fury of the incoming Atlantic

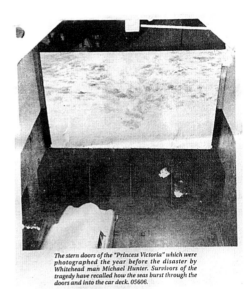

The stern doors of the "Princess Victoria" which were photographed the year before the disaster by Whitehead man Michael Hunter. Survivors of the tragedy have recalled how the seas burst through the doors and into the car deck. 05606.

A view of the open stern doors of the *Princess Victoria*, taken in 1952 from the aft docking deck.

*Larne Times*

The officers of the *Princess Victoria* in 1947: from the left, Third Officer William McInnes, Radio Operator David Broadfoot, Captain James Ferguson, Chief Officer Shirley Duckels and Second Officer Leslie Unsworth (who did not travel on the ship).

*Wigtown Free Press*

gale, attempted to steer on a northerly course and use the coast of Scotland to give some shelter before making an attempt to turn the ship in order to try and re-enter the loch. This action was to place the Achilles heel of the ship – the stern doors and the open space above them – into a position that directly exposed them to the very heavy seas.

As the ship turned she was hit by an exceptionally heavy sea. On board the waves crashed over the ship, hitting as far forward as the galley roof, situated well forward on that deck. On the car deck McQuiston was standing on the turntable when the sea hit the ship and burst open the stern doors, the force of the water carrying away the slip bolts and upright stays that were holding the doors shut. The water quickly rushed into the car deck to a depth of nearly one and a half feet, knocking McQuiston off his feet. On the boat deck passenger James Wallace was standing at the stern and watched as the sea came in through the doors, ripping and bending the struts of the stern doors in its path. Initially around 200 tons or approximately 44,000 gallons of water had entered the car deck, and with the doors now open the whole of the car deck, even though it was 11 feet above sea level, was vulnerable to continued flooding.

In the lounge, the passengers were tossed about as the ship was hit by the heavy wave. Sir Walter Smiles and Ernest Flack were thrown out of their chairs; Maynard Sinclair, who had been sitting at a table, was thrown completely out of his seat and right over the table. Steward James Blair assisted the gentlemen back into their seats, but Sir Walter was on his hands and knees and was looking for his glasses. He wished to sit on the floor and Blair placed a cushion under him. With weather conditions so bad it is not surprising that a great many of the passengers were starting to feel the first effects of seasickness, and were making for the toilets. One passenger, John Stanford, to this day still remembers the sound and smell of people being violently seasick in the ship.

On the bridge Captain Ferguson had Chief Officer Duckels dispatched to the car deck to ascertain what damage had been caused. When Duckels arrived what lay before him was a deck flooded and completely open to the sea, which was washing in and out with the continued push of the waves. The scuppers, the holes in the side of the deck designed to drain it of any spillage, were unable to cope with the vast volume of water. Mail bags and packets were being tossed about by the water and some of the bags were being washed out of the open stern into the Irish Sea. The gale with its hurricane force was continuing to pound at the ship.

Duckels was joined by the ship's Second Officer Leonard White, and between them they organised an attempt by some of the crew to try to close the rear doors. John Murdoch, John Garrett, Willie Mann and William McCarlie were assembled on the car deck to undertake this dangerous task. Able Seaman Alec Craig had a rope tied around his middle to save him being washed away as

An artist's impression of the attempt by Able Seaman Alec Craig to close the breached stern car deck doors.

*BBC Northern Ireland*

he made his way to the open doors. Using crowbars, the crew tried for a period of time to get the doors to close over. By this time the water was about a foot deep on the deck. Between them they managed to get the starboard door about a third of the way closed, but the port-side door would not move for them. The remainder of the crew members, assembled earlier by Duckels, tried to move some of the cargo to the doors in an attempt to brace the doors with the weight of whatever cargo they could move, but this also proved fruitless. Large amounts of water were now freely moving in and out and around the car deck and the cargo was gradually starting to move towards the starboard side. The attempt to close the doors was finally abandoned after about 20 minutes.

On the bridge Captain Ferguson was placed in a terrible quandary. The stern of the ship was now totally open to the waves; if he did not attempt to turn the ship and give some shelter or protection to the exposed rear of the vessel, the car deck would continue to flood and the stability of the ship would be lost, with potential

An artist's impression of the moments after the rear doors were burst open by the sea.

*John Bull Magazine*

disastrous consequences for all on board. Only one course of action lay open to him, and that was to turn the ship and reverse, stern first, back into the comparative calmness and safety of Loch Ryan. This action would allow the open aft deck to be given some protection from the continuing flow of the sea and the pounding of the waves. For the ship to be driven in reverse would require that the bow rudder be engaged and that would mean crew members having to go forward to the exposed forecastle head of the ship in this force 12 gale. If it could be released, the rudder, which was located and locked in place in the bow of the ship, would allow the vessel to navigate safely while going astern.

Able Seaman Angus Nelson, along with McKinnon and William Gowan, the ship's carpenter, were ordered to go forward to the forecastle head at the bow of the ship and attempt to remove the locking gear and engage the bow rudder. As they made their way forward, the waves were breaking over the bow of the ship. The three of them managed to get to the rudder-releasing wheel, but with the sea breaking over them it was becoming extremely dangerous to stay where they were. Nelson later stated that Captain Ferguson waved at them and beckoned them to come back to safety. The failure to release the rudder and safely return to Loch Ryan, and the fact that the ship's engines were still running and propelling the ship forward, was to spell disaster for all on board. By now the time was just after 09.30 and the first sign to the authorities of the perilous position of the *Princess Victoria* was about to be made known; surprisingly, however, a distress message was not broadcast.

At 09.46 David Broadfoot in his radio cabin was handed a message that he, like all seafaring radio operators, would most probably have hoped he would never have to send, a message that their vessel was in difficulties. But this message did not fully reflect the position that the ship and those on board her were in, as it was only a 'triple X', signifying an urgent as opposed to the more familiar distress SOS message. Quickly and methodically Broadfoot tapped out the message to Portpatrick Radio on his Morse key: "*Princess Victoria* to GPK-X.X.X. Hove to off mouth of Loch Ryan. Vessel not under command. Urgent assistance of tug required." Within a few minutes he was again sending another message, this time a private communication to the ship's owners, British Railways, at Stranraer: "09.56 Hove to, vessel not under command, have asked for immediate assistance of tug. Signed Ferguson."

The ship, which by now had developed at list of around 15 degrees, was still under power and sailing on a northwesterly course. By the time the first message was transmitted, the ship was positioned some seven to eight miles to the north-west of the mouth of Loch Ryan. The inaccuracy of the crew in plotting their position was to cause the Coastguard and rescue craft involved in the search to believe that the *Princess Victoria* was closer to the Scottish coast than she actually was.

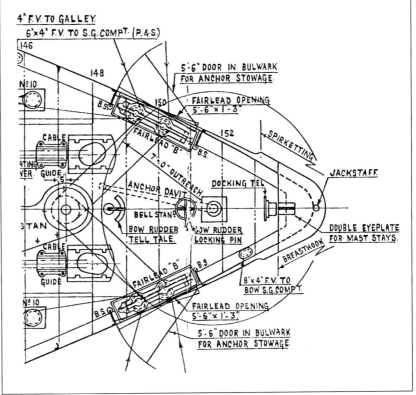

Plan view of the forecastle head showing the locking pin for the bow rudder. *PRONI*

# *The call for 5 assistance*

Her Majesty's Coastguard station at Portpatrick and Portpatrick Radio station are housed in two separate buildings overlooking the Irish Sea, slightly to the north of Portpatrick on the Rinns Peninsula. On the morning of 31 January 1953 William McGregor was the officer in charge at the radio station, which was licensed and operated for the government by the Post Office. The two radio operators on duty that morning were Sam Batte, who was on radio watch, and William Ross, who was on Morse code watch. The call sign for Portpatrick Radio station was GPK.

Twenty yards from the radio station was the building that housed the Coastguard. In charge on that morning was Station Officer David T McGarrie. These two separate buildings had no direct communication with each other. Messages that were received by the radio station had to be written down and then taken physically to the Coastguard building. When the Coastguard wished a message transmitted, the text was written down and then physically taken to the radio station for transmission. As the events of the day unfolded there were to be many problems of communication between these agencies, with much valuable time lost. Under the conditions of the Post Office Operating Licence the operators at the radio station were not permitted to transmit any information on their own initiative – they could only transmit messages that were passed to them by the Coastguard.

One other major problem, that these two organisations would be faced with on this terrible day, was the fact that the *Princess Victoria* could only communicate in Morse code, whilst all the other ships and land stations involved in the rescue attempt were only able to communicate with each other in speech on radio telephone. Only HMS *Contest*, the Royal Navy destroyer, and Portpatrick Radio would be able to work in both wireless (Morse code) and radio (speech) telegraphy. This double radio traffic would add greatly to the burden of the two operators at Portpatrick Radio station. When a message was received from the *Princess Victoria* it had to be written down and

District Officer William Spreadborough and Mr McGarrie of the Portpatrick Coastguard station.    *Wigtown Free Press*

then passed to the Coastguard. There would then be a delay while the Coastguard would decide what action was to be taken. This new message would then have to be taken to the radio station and rebroadcast for all the rescue ships to hear.

Batte in the radio station took the first triple XXX message, received at 09.47, and passed it to his superior, William McGregor. The latter then had the message passed to the Coastguard in their adjacent building, as well as having copies sent to the Admiralty at Plymouth, Lloyd's in London and the local Lloyd's agent at Stranraer. In the Coastguard building Station Officer McGarrie telephoned his District Officer, William Spreadborough, who made his way immediately to take charge of the situation. Portpatrick Radio rebroadcast the assistance message received from the *Princess Victoria* two minutes later as a 'CQ' ('all ships') message.

When the message arrived with the Coastguard, Spreadborough contacted George Sutherland at Corsewall Point Lighthouse and also Cairnryan Lighthouse to determine if the ship could be seen. Both locations replied that at 10.00 they could not see the ship. Spreadborough initiated a message to be sent to the

*Princess Victoria* which read: "Please indicate your position now, do you require lifeboat or LSA [life saving appliances] now." This was sent at 10.18, 18 minutes after receipt of the initial XXX message.

At 10.22 the Coastguard sent a message for assistance to the Royal Navy. The nearest vessel that could assist was the 2,515-ton destroyer HMS *Contest*, anchored at Rothesay. It would take at least one hour for her to be at full readiness. At 10.26 Mr Walker from the Portpatrick lifeboat contacted the Coastguard and said that he would assemble a crew, word of the plight of the ship having started to filter out.

At 10.30 the Admiralty steam tug *Salveda* called Portpatrick Radio to say that they had overheard the earlier call for assistance from the *Princess Victoria*. This tug, captained by Malcolm Anderson, had left the Clyde earlier in the morning and was approximately 20 miles north-west off Corsewall Point and proceeding for the Isle of Lewis to assist another vessel in distress. She informed Portpatrick that she would immediately alter course to Corsewall Point.

Meanwhile, back in the British Railways offices at Stranraer, John Maxwell was in charge that morning due to the illness of the Senior Clerk David Stuart. Maxwell had received the private message of 09.45 stating that the ship was four miles off Corsewall and required assistance. The local Lloyd's agent, Mr Bingham, was informed and Maxwell asked if Bingham could secure tugs to assist. He also contacted Cairnryan port to see if they could assist, but the ocean-going tugs that had been at Cairnryan had left a few days earlier. Maxwell was told

that a cargo steamer, the *Campbell*, was at Cairnryan and that it would be sent to assist once it had raised steam. British Railways headquarters at Euston station in London were also informed at about 09.55.

At Portpatrick Radio station the time was approaching 10.43 when the radio operators received the first SOS message from the *Princess Victoria*: "*Princess Victoria* to SOS. – *Princess Victoria* four miles north-west of Corsewall. Car-deck flooded. Heavy list to starboard. Require immediate assistance. Ship not under command." The nearest tugs that could be of assistance were the *Brigadier* and *Warrior* which were both sheltering off Douglas Bay in the Isle of Man. Within two minutes the Coastguard requested the Portpatrick lifeboat to launch to the assistance of the *Princess Victoria*.

At Portpatrick, the Coxswain William McConnell had been contacted earlier, at about 10.20, by Mr Walker who was deputising for the Honorary Secretary. Walker told him of the plight of the *Princess Victoria* and McConnell, who had recently resigned from the position as coxswain of the lifeboat, made his way down to the lifeboat station to assemble the crew when the maroon was fired calling on the crew to respond. The fact that no successor had to date been appointed to take over the duties of coxswain did not stop McConnell making his way to the lifeboat station to take command in response to this call for help. Within minutes he was joined by Second Coxswain William Hunter, James Mitchell the engineer, William McKie, John Smith, James Alexander and Adam and James Rankin, who all made ready the lifeboat, the *Jeanie Speirs*, for immediate launch. The lifeboat, a

HMS *Contest*, based in Scotland, was the first ship to respond to the call for assistance.

*Royal Navy*

The *Jeanie Speirs*, the lifeboat based at Portpatrick.

*Q Nelson collection*

Watson class, was 46 feet in length with a speed of 8¼ knots. She was also equipped with radio telephone and could carry up to 90 passengers. The *Jeanie Speirs* was launched into the hurricane force conditions at 11.00 and headed on a northerly course to try and intercept the *Princess Victoria* at her last given position of four miles north-west of Corsewall Point.

Sixty miles to the north of Corsewall Point, at Rothesay on the Isle of Bute, preparations were well under way to have the destroyer HMS *Contest* made ready for sea. The main problem facing her commanding officer, Lieutenant Commander Harvey Fleming, and his crew of ten officers and 130 ratings, was the distance that they were from the *Princess Victoria* at her estimated position off Corsewall Point and the mountainous seas that separated them. Steam was finally raised and the destroyer set sail from Rothesay at 11.09, with full speed on both boilers reached at 11.25. The ship initially proceeded at 32 knots but was rolling at up to 40 degrees. Waves of up to 30 feet in height and winds of up to 70 knots were experienced, necessitating the speed being reduced to 15 knots. Some minor damage was caused on the upper deck to a dingy store and depth charge rack and two ratings suffered minor injuries as the ship proceeded south.

Earlier, at 10.34, HMS *Contest* received a distress call in Morse from the *Princess Victoria*, giving her position as four miles north-west of Corsewall Point and stating that her car deck was flooded, with a heavy list to starboard, that she was not under control and required immediate assistance. On the bridge of the destroyer,

Fleming calculated that they would not reach the *Princess Victoria*'s position until 13.00. A message was sent to the stricken passenger ferry asking for details on the degree of the flooding, her list, and her voltage. Arrangements were made on HMS *Contest* to pump oil onto the sea if required. Fleming's plan was that when he arrived on the scene, he would, if possible, get a pump on board, take the ship in tow and head for the safety of Luce Bay, to the south of Portpatrick. The race against the clock and the elements was now on to save those on board the *Princess Victoria*.

On the other side of the Irish Sea, in the Harbour Commissioners' building in Belfast, Captain Alfred Robinson received a signal at 10.34 from the Royal Naval Operations base at Londonderry to the effect that there was an emergency with the *Princess Victoria* off Corsewall Point, and requesting if the Belfast Harbour Commissioners had a tug available to assist. There were several tugs in dock in Belfast, but none of these were ocean-going and after contacting the Lloyd's agent in Stranraer it was decided that, with the emergency on the Scottish side of the Irish Sea, there was little assistance that Belfast could offer. The only other offer of assistance that Belfast could give was in the form of the Heysham ferry the *Duke of Argyll*, which was berthed in Belfast. The crew of the vessel had been discharged, with only a skeleton crew on board and according to her master, Alfred Wilmott, it would take three hours to get the ship ready for sea and then a further journey time of three hours to get to Corsewall Point.

In Belfast Lough several ships were gathering to seek shelter and ride out the storm in the comparative safety that these sheltered waters would give. The first to arrive was the MV *Lairdsmoor*, a cargo vessel with 112 tons of general cargo and 100 head of cattle on board. Her captain was James Bell. The *Lairdsmoor* had left Dublin, bound for Glasgow, at 18.00 on the previous evening and at about 02.10 in the morning of 31 January, whilst passing Black Head at the northern entrance to Belfast Lough, encountered a very heavy sea with poor visibility caused by showers of hail. Bell decided to proceed further north, but as the weather was worsening he returned to Belfast Lough and dropped anchor at 07.30. At around 09.50 Bell again decided to carry on his journey and proceeded to weigh anchor and then to steam northwards, but again because the weather was so bad he was forced to return to the lough, arriving at 11.55.

Skipper David Brewster was in charge of the trawler *Eastcoates*. The vessel was a 277-ton fishing boat and had left Fleetwood heading for the fishing grounds to the west of Scotland on the Friday evening. Like Bell of the *Lairdsmoor*, Brewster also encountered heavy seas and a gale when passing the Mull of Galloway and decided to run for the shelter of Belfast Lough, arriving there at around 06.30 hours.

The third ship that was to anchor at the entrance to Belfast Lough was the oil tanker the *Pass of Drumochter*. Under the command of Captain James Kelly, the tanker had left Belfast bound for Stanlow at 09.45 and arrived near the other two vessels, dropping her anchor at around 10.50 hours. Kelly's intention was to ballast his vessel and then to proceed on his journey.

Steaming out of Belfast harbour a few hours behind the *Pass of Drumochter*, bound for Glasgow, was the cargo vessel the *Orchy*, captained by Hugh Matheson, a native of the Isle of Skye. By the time the *Orchy* arrived at Black Head, the weather was so bad that after attempting to proceed, her captain decided to return to the lough and weigh anchor until the storm passed.

The *Lairdsmoor* and *Eastcoates* were seeking refuge in Belfast Lough as the *Princess Victoria* was about to start her final voyage and as the radio messages from the stricken ship to Portpatrick Radio were being broadcast. The ships in Belfast Lough were listening in to the radio messages as they were rebroadcast from Portpatrick, but with the severity of the weather and the distance that they were from the Scottish coast, and the knowledge from radio broadcasts at 10.30 hours that a tug was proceeding to the assistance of the stricken ship, there was very little they could do.

Their role in the rescue mission was to come within a few short hours, when their captains realised just how close the *Princess Victoria* was to them. As events unfolded, these crews were to play a major role in the rescue of those that were to survive the horrors ahead.

# *The journey 6 continues*

Captain Ferguson had one last chance to save the ship and those on board, and that was to try to turn his vessel around and head back into Loch Ryan. Following the earlier unsuccessful attempt to release the bow rudder, he was left with no other plan of action, because to stay where he was would lead to the ship continuing to take a pounding from the sea which she would not survive. He tried to manoeuvre the ship back to the loch but as soon as the vessel turned, the wind and waves were crashing against the port side causing the list on the starboard side to increase initially to around 40 to 50 degrees. There was now a real danger of the ship capsizing.

**10.00 hours**

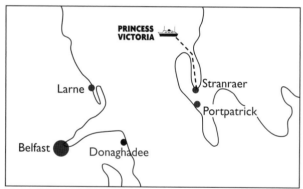

The following series of maps are not to scale.

By now the *Princess Victoria* was almost seven miles to the north-north-east of Corsewall Point, the most northerly point that it would reach. The flimsy stern doors of the ship had been breached by the waves and the car deck was now awash with sea water, freely flowing in and out through the doors. When the first wave had struck the ship it also broke a window in the third class lounge and water was also entering into the passenger accommodation. Conditions for the passengers and crew were terrible, with the ship developing a list and continuing to be buffeted by the sea. Many of them were experiencing the worst seasickness that they had ever had. On the bridge, Captain Ferguson, realising then that

there was no way back for him, took the very brave decision to try, even with the list on the ship, to make a dash across the Irish Sea to the safety of Larne. At around 10.00 the *Princess Victoria* was turned to try to head eastwards. There was one major problem that faced Ferguson: as the list to starboard side increased, the eight-foot diameter port propeller was raised towards the surface of the water, reducing the driving force of that blade and making it extremely difficult to accurately steer the ship. With the driving force of the port propeller diminishing, the ship would begin to adopt a position where as it was moving forward it would be lower in the water on the starboard side and would veer in that direction.

While these problems were being faced on the bridge of the *Princess Victoria*, the passengers and crew were also facing a harrowing time inside the ship. Around 10.00 Able Seaman John Murdoch was in the lower lounge and decided to open the door between the lounge and the car deck on the starboard side to see what was going on. When the door was opened he could clearly see that about half of the car deck was covered with water to a depth of over a foot; as he looked further aft he could see some of his shipmates busy at the stern of the car deck desperately trying to close the doors. He closed the door and made his way to the damaged stern doors to try

An artist's impression of the crew's attempts to shore up the damaged rear car-deck doors.   *BBC Northern Ireland*

and assist. Within a few minutes the ship had developed quite a heavy list to starboard. Murdoch was then ordered to go to the bridge to relieve one of the lookouts, and while there, had a conversation with the quartermaster who said that there was no difficulty steering the ship.

The door through which Murdoch made his way onto the car deck, whilst still closed was, however, not watertight. As the list in the ship increased so the water level on the car deck increased and rose above the sill of the door, starting to seep into the lounge. As the water level rose it began to enter the engine room and the compartments on the lower deck via this door and the ventilator pipes on the car deck.

In the third class lounge, British Railway fireman John Fitzpatrick noticed, along with the other passengers, that he had to hold on to his seat or else he would have slid off it. Around 10.00 he heard the first of many announcements given from the bridge. Over the public address system the passengers were told: "Your attention everyone. The captain asks you to be prepared for heavy rolling. The ship is going through a severe test, but there is no danger. You are quite safe." This message did help to give some sort of reassurance as there were no reports of any panic at this early stage.

By 10.30 the ship had developed such a list that the sea was clearly visible out of the starboard windows in the lounge. Any furniture in the lower lounges that was not secured was by this stage sliding across the decks towards the starboard side of the ship, and walking about was becoming very difficult for the passengers.

At 10.32 in the radio room behind the bridge, Broadfoot began transmitting in Morse code the first distress call from the ship:

> Princess Victoria to SOS. – Princess Victoria four miles north-west of Corsewall. Car-deck flooded. Heavy list to starboard. Require immediate assistance. Ship not under command.

On receipt of the message Portpatrick Radio transmitted a CQ to all listening stations informing them of the *Princess Victoria*'s distress message.

The water that had earlier entered the lower lounge from the car deck as just a seepage was now almost filling half of the deck in some places, to a depth of between one and one and a half feet. Some of the crew tried for a short period of time to bale the water out, but this was proving to be a useless exercise and in the end the chief steward gave instructions to stop.

## 11.00 hours

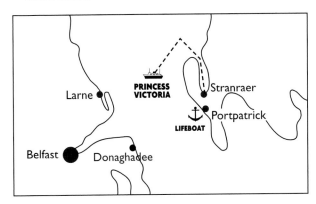

At 11.00, nine miles to the east of the *Princess Victoria*, the Portpatrick lifeboat, the *Jeanie Speirs*, was launched. The crew had been told that the ship was to the north-west of Corsewall Point, and set a course for that position. Unknown to Coxswain William McConnell and his crew, by now the *Princess Victoria* had drifted to the south of Corsewall Point and around this time was heading into the middle of the North Channel. Her bearing was now north-west of Portpatrick and not Corsewall Point. If McConnell had known this and sailed in an westerly direction, he would have come across the ship in less than an hour. As it was, the Portpatrick lifeboat wasted valuable time proceeding northwards until, much later in the day, it was realised that the *Princess Victoria* was further south.

Shortly after 11.00, on A deck, Chief Officer Duckels made an announcement using a loud hailer. He informed the passengers that the ship was passing through a difficult time, that they were to remain calm and would be supplied with life jackets. Many of the crew were dispatched to hand out the life jackets and also to assist the passengers in donning them. At around the same time Duckels also gave orders for some of the able seamen on the ship to start preparing the lifeboats for launching. This proved to be extremely difficult as, due to the rolling of the ship, the lifeboats on the starboard side were touching the water. The crew working on the boats carried on with their preparations, but in some of the boats the oars and some of the smaller gear stowed in

An artist's impression of the passengers discussing the precarious position they are in. *BBC Northern Ireland*

them were washed away. This lack of oars would later add to the problems of trying to navigate the lifeboats and rescue survivors from the water. Steward James Blair came across Stewardesses Mary Close and Roseann Baxter who had John and Kevin Mooney with them. Their mother was in the dining room and the two stewardesses were trying to get life jackets to fit the children. Blair and fellow Steward James McCowan got jackets and put them on the two children before they went back to their mother.

At 11.10 Captain Ferguson instructed that a second private message be sent to the ship's owners, British Railways, at Stranraer to inform them of the current position:

Have sent distress call; 4 miles North West Corsewall; car deck flooded; heavy list to starboard; require immediate assistance; ship not under control.

No reply was sent, but British Railways headquarters at Euston in London was informed by the Stranraer office.

To the north, HMS *Contest* had finally raised steam and was now ready to proceed to the rescue. The destroyer was under way at 11.09, with an estimated time of arrival at Corsewall of 13.00.

On the bridge of the *Princess Victoria* a discussion took place on how to try and reduce the amount of water that was freely flowing about on the car deck. The rear doors would not close and the crew on the deck had tried to clear the scuppers on the starboard side, but with the

shift in the cargo it was impossible to get anywhere near them. It was finally decided that an attempt should be made to open the port sliding hull doors, and the Second Officer Leonard White assembled Able Seaman Murdoch, Ship's Carpenter William Gowan and Bosun William McCarlie with instructions that they should go and standby. The three of them made their way down to the car deck with orders to release the bolts holding the door shut. This order was then quickly cancelled by the deck officers and the bolts were tightened again. What the ship's officers were trying to accomplish is uncertain. With the list in the ship by now so pronounced, the starboard cargo doors were level on the outside of the hull with the sea. The port door on the opposite side of the car deck was well above the water line and it would therefore have been impossible for water to drain uphill across the car deck and out of the port door. By now the starboard stern quarter was under a continuous pounding by the waves and almost completely submerged. The list in the ship was now around 30 degrees.

At around 11.30 another announcement was made over the ship's tannoy system. This message was not as reassuring as the previous one because, firstly, it was given by the captain and, secondly, it informed those on board that the ship was passing through a period of grave emergency and that life jackets would be issued to all passengers.

Passenger Billy Copley had just awoken from a sleep in his bunk. He had joined the ship at around midnight and had gone straight to his cabin and quickly fallen asleep. Similarly James Kerr, a sea captain who was master of one of Kelly's coal boats, had also joined the ship around the same time as Copley and, like him, had gone to his cabin. Kerr, an experienced seafarer, had slept through the initial storm. But when both men awoke and got out of their bunks what greeted them sent a chill down their spines. The ship by now was listing very badly to starboard, Kerr estimating it to be about 45 degrees.

At 11.35 Radio Officer David Broadfoot was in the process of broadcasting to Portpatrick Radio the third distress message from the ship:

Princess Victoria GMZN. Position approximately five miles WNW from Corsewall. Car-deck flooded. Very heavy list to starboard. Ship not under command. Require immediate assistance.

This message, like many that emanated from the ship, showed that the captain and bridge officers did not fully appreciate where they actually were in relation to Corsewall Point. By the time the 11.35 message was sent, the *Princess Victoria* was still under power and moving south. Her actual position now was roughly eight miles west-south-west of Corsewall and not five miles west-north-west as stated in the distress message. The ship was approximately ten miles further to the south of the given position, and the rescue vessels – the *Jeanie Speirs*, HMS *Contest* and the tug *Salveda* – were then altering their courses to make for that location. Still under power, the *Princess Victoria* was moving further south by the minute. Another vessel, the *Nurani*, had answered the call from Portpatrick Radio for assistance, but this ship was 100 miles to the south and could only proceed at 6 knots. Portpatrick Radio, using their D/F (direction finding) equipment, had half an hour earlier taken a bearing on the *Princess Victoria* while the ship was transmitting to try and determine the ship's position. No other station at that time was able to get a second or cross-bearing and the reading of 316 degrees from Portpatrick could therefore not be relied upon as a true fix. Two bearings were needed to pinpoint the exact location of the ship, but this bearing of 316 degrees did show that the ship was further south than she was suggesting in the distress messages. No action was taken on the bearing read by Portpatrick Radio.

At 11.43 the *Princess Victoria* received a message from HMS *Contest*:

> To Princess Victoria GMZN from Warship Contest GGWP Am proceeding to your assistance with all dispatch Stop ETA 13.00. Z Request details of extent of flooding and list. Have you power? If so, voltage AC or DC.

News of the progress of *Contest* quickly spread throughout the ship and some passengers were told that the destroyer would be with them by 13.00.

On board HMS *Contest*, Lieutenant Commander Harvey Fleming had been steaming south from Rothesay. The destroyer was maintaining a speed of 32 knots, but because of the heavy seas the vessel was rolling at up to 40 degrees, and speed had to be reduced. As previously mentioned, Fleming's plan was twofold: firstly he had arrangements made on *Contest* to pump oil onto the sea when they approached the *Princess Victoria*;

secondly, his main intention was to take the stricken ship in tow and proceed to enter Loch Ryan. If the ship had shifted southward, Fleming planned to take her to Luce Bay, which would have been more sheltered. From a distance, and considering the messages received, Fleming felt that while the situation was serious it was not critical, as the ferry was, according to her messages, lying off the entrance to Loch Ryan. This assessment of the situation was to change when the *Princess Victoria* replied at 11.57 to the earlier message from *Contest*:

> SOS GGWP Warship Contest 35 degrees list to starboard approximately 200 tons water and cargo in car-deck Power 220 volts DC 123 passengers 60 crew approx. 5 miles W by S of Corsewall. Master GMZN.

This was the first indication to the rescue services and vessels that the ship was moving southwards faster than expected. The number of people referred to as on board the *Princess Victoria* is also at variance with the figure quoted at the subsequent Inquiry and also my research.

**12.00 hours**

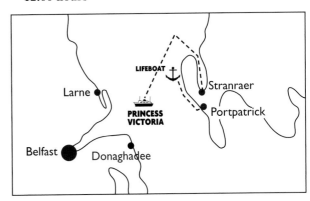

By now the ship was about 11 miles west-south-west of Corsewall Point. At the lighthouse on the Point, keeper George Sutherland was still keeping watch for any sight of the ship and at this time he saw the tug *Salveda* about three miles off the coast, heading in a southerly direction.

In the saloon of the *Princess Victoria*, passenger John Fitzpatrick noticed that the clock stopped working at ten minutes past twelve; it started working again, but at twenty-five minutes past noon, stopped working for good. The list in the ship was by now becoming so pronounced that as the ship rolled sidewards the windows in the third class saloon were under the surface of the water. Steward James Blair was assisting the passengers, who were mostly gathered in the lounge, the smoke room and some on the port promenade deck, in donning their life jackets. After this he made his way past the bridge and met Captain Ferguson. They had known each other for many years and the captain asked Blair how things were down below. Blair informed him that the smoke room was a bit of a shambles, but that no passenger had been injured. Ferguson then instructed Blair to try and keep the passengers as near the doors as possible, because things were serious. He also informed Blair that there were two tugs and a navy destroyer en route to their assistance and that they should arrive by 13.00.

Blair made his way to the bureau office on the promenade deck and told some of the passengers of his conversation with the captain. At the bureau he was met by the chief steward who asked for lifelines to be set out and run down the stairs to the deck below and then run out to the doors, to give the passengers something to hold on to as they tried to get up to the deck. The list was now so great that when the lines were being laid out Blair noticed that many of the passengers had slid down the deck to the corners of the entrance hall. He and another steward, Gerald Morgan, slid down the sloping deck, tied a line around the passengers and climbed back up the line. They hauled the passengers up to the port side of the ship. Passenger Nancy Bryson was close by. Her handbag had slipped from her grasp and was lying at the starboard side of the ship. She was in quite a state of panic following the loss of her bag, so Morgan slid across the

An artist's impression of the passengers trying to get to safety, moving through the darkened and listing ship.

*BBC Northern Ireland*

deck and managed to retrieve and return it.

Another passenger, Joseph Hastings, started to haul himself up one of the lines that had been laid out, but managed to get his hand caught. Fortunately, he carried a small pen knife in his pocket and had to use this to free his hand, before pulling himself up the line to the deck.

Steward Charles Thompson was approached by several passengers who asked if he could go down to their cabins and retrieve their coats. Thompson made his way down to C deck and while recovering the coats, saw that there was now about two feet of water in the side of the ship in the passage ways.

The sea continued relentlessly to pound and batter against the vessel, especially at the vulnerable stern, pushing the starboard quarter further into the water. The weather was between force 9 and 12, giving waves of at least 13.5 metres high. The list in the ship was by now 35 degrees.

At Portpatrick Coastguard there was now a major effort underway to try and establish the true position of the *Princess Victoria*. At 12.00, for six minutes, Broadfoot, on the ship, had transmitted a series of single letter 'Vs'. This sending of 'V' in Morse code, which is "...-", was an established method to allow other radio stations to obtain a bearing on the direction that the signal was coming from. When two receiving stations could each obtain a bearing and these bearings were transposed to a map, the position of the sender could be identified. The *Princess Victoria* also started her radar equipment to try and get a bearing on HMS *Contest*. At 12.17 Malin Head Radio station in the Republic of Ireland had a confirmed bearing of 112.5 degrees, while Portpatrick was also able to determine a bearing of 282 degrees. When these bearings were transposed to a map, the position where they crossed would indicate the ship's position. What a shock William Spreadborough at the Coastguard in Portpatrick must have got when it was clearly shown that the ferry was now much further south that had been understood, based on the information that the vessel was giving. This new information now placed the *Princess Victoria* less than 12 miles to the north-north-east of Mew Island, part of the Copeland Islands group off the Donaghadee coast of Northern Ireland. More worrying was the realisation that the ship was now 16 miles further to the south of her previously stated position off Corsewall Point at the entrance to Loch Ryan. Unnoticed, the *Princess Victoria* had by now nearly crossed the Irish Sea.

Within a few minutes the *Princess Victoria* transmitted:

Princess Victoria to GGWP [Contest] and GPK [Portpatrick] Approx. position 280 degrees seven miles from Killantringan. Posn grave but list not appreciably worsening.

Killantringan is about one and a half miles to the north of Portpatrick, but this position as given by the ship was wrong. The previous confirmed bearings from Malin Head and Portpatrick placed the ship a further three and a half miles to the west. With this information, HMS *Contest* had to recalculate its time of arrival at the updated location. It was now going to take the destroyer at least a further 45 minutes to reach the ship. Portpatrick could see that the two positions – the ship's and the cross-bearings – were several miles apart and immediately contacted the ship to ask what was their approximate position off the Scottish coast. The reply sent by Broadfoot at 12.47 was of no help: "Sorry Radar no use to[o] much list."

On the ship the situation was now becoming extremely critical. With a list of 35 degrees there could be anything up to 500 tons of water (almost 120,000 gallons) on the car deck, to a depth of over four feet. As this water was unable to drain away, it then seeped deeper into the ship's hull. This had the effect of pushing the ship deeper and deeper into the water, a position that it would be impossible to recover from. It also allowed the waves to freely wash over the whole stern of the ship, driving this part of the vessel even further into the water.

The list was now so pronounced that those on board had great difficulty in moving about – the walls were starting to become the floor as they tried to make their way to the higher port-side of the ship. At 12.52 the *Princess Victoria* transmitted the following:

Posn. critical starboard engine room flooded.

There was now no possibility that the ship could be saved. The *Princess Victoria* was now entering its final hours and the fate of those on board would depend on their strength and determination, and the efforts of the crew.

**13.00 hours**

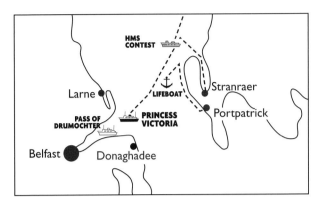

The list in the ship was by now so steep that it was impossible to walk around the vessel. The lifelines that had been laid from the bureau to the port side of the promenade deck were now being used by passengers to haul themselves to the open deck and the highest part of the ship. The men and crew were helping women and children to drag themselves upwards in response to an announcement from the bridge that all passengers should get as high as possible in the vessel. James Carlin helped his wife Eileen and her sister Marie up to the boat deck. He then when back down into the ship to their cabins to find his mother-in-law Mary Connery. He brought her up to the boat deck as well. By this time, with the force of the waves, the ship was listing up to about 60 degrees, but Carlin had nonetheless managed to get the whole family together on the sloping deck.

Another message was broadcast over the tannoy telling the passengers that a navy destroyer was coming to their aid and would be with them in about 15 minutes. As the ship lurched and was buffeted by the waves, the passengers were also being tossed around inside the ship. One man fell against the purser's office and cut his face badly. Another lady was making her way towards the open deck carrying two small bags, and passed Robert Baillie; he managed to pull her up until she was able to grasp onto the purser's office. This lady refused to move any further saying, "When you get to my age you are too old for this." She also said that the bags that she was clinging to contained "all the money I have in the world". (Later the body of this unidentified lady was recovered. In the bags she was clutching were bank notes to the value of over £900.)

In the entrance hall, where the bureau was situated, water was now starting to enter through the outer hull door from the starboard side. A steward was trying to block the door at the side to keep the water out. Stewards Blair and Ross organised some passengers to assist others who were still in the entrance hall. Using a rope, seven men and three women were hauled up to the deck on their stomachs as the list was so severe that they could not crawl up to the deck from the side of the stairway. One man slipped before the rope was tied around him; he fell back and hit the starboard side of the ship. Eventually he was hauled back up, but broke his leg due to the fall and his life jacket was covered in blood. Passenger Annie Jackson, assisted by Maynard Sinclair, was also helping some of the mothers on the ship who were trying to get their children up to the deck.

At 13.08 the engine room was flooded and the engines stopped. On the bridge Captain Ferguson, realising how far the ship had now travelled and how close they were to the Irish coast, spoke to Second Engineer John Taylor. He asked if it was possible to get the engines restarted to try to make a quick dash to the more sheltered waters off the nearby coastline. Taylor replied that the engine room was too badly flooded – by now the funnel of the ship was dipping into the waves. At the same time another message was sent from the ship to Portpatrick Radio:

SOS Now stopped ship on her beam ends HW.

Back on the promenade deck some of the passengers who were clinging onto the rails noticed through the side windows that some people were still in the lounge. There was no possible escape for them through the main entrance. One steward took a fire hose and with the brass nozzle, broke one of the lounge windows. A rope was found and quickly lowered into the upturned lounge. Passenger Ivor Thomas dragged a 30-year-old woman through the window. A man who was hanging onto a table was also hauled to the comparative safety of the deck, and an old lady was also rescued. This lady had no shoes or life jacket on and Thomas gave her his life jacket. James Wallace and John Ross passed women and children from the lounge up to those outside, finally making their own way out onto the exposed deck.

In another part of the lounge, Albert Dickie and his friend Robert Deans were standing beside a steward who smashed another window. Dickie used his greatcoat as

padding over the broken glass and both of them hauled themselves out. Before they made their way to the deck, they helped pull several other passengers up through the broken window.

At his home in Donaghadee, Hugh Nelson, the 63-year-old coxswain of the local lifeboat the *Sir Samuel Kelly*, was listening to the BBC radio news. Nelson had been a crew member of the lifeboat since 1910 and for the last four years had had the honour of being the coxswain. On hearing the news of the critical position of the *Princess Victoria*, he and his son, also called Hugh, made their way down to the harbour in Donaghadee where the lifeboat was moored. The lifeboat was a Watson class, built in 1950 at the Isle of Wight. Her top speed was 8 knots and her length was almost 47 feet. The boat was designed to hold a crew of eight, while she could accommodate 95 passengers. At 13.25 Nelson senior received a message from David McKibbin, the Honorary Secretary at Donaghadee, to say that there was a vessel in distress between Portpatrick and Donaghadee requiring immediate assistance. Within a few minutes the maroons were fired to alert the rest of the crew and at 13.40 the lifeboat, crewed by Hugh Nelson and son Hugh, Alex, Frank and William Nelson, Samuel Herron, George Lindsay and Engineer James Armstrong, was making its way out of the sheltered harbour at Donaghadee on a journey that would see the crew and lifeboat at sea for over 24 of the next 36 hours. Coxswain Hugh Nelson was to be continuously at the helm in the open cockpit of his vessel for the next four hours. When the lifeboat was under way she contacted the Coastguard at Portpatrick and was informed to proceed to a position five miles east of Mew Island. (Crew members John Trimble and Sammy Nelson were out of town and missed the initial call-out, but they would help crew the vessel later that day.)

At 13.15 the *Princess Victoria* informed Portpatrick:

We are preparing to abandon ship.

The crew was well into the procedure for making the lifeboats ready for launching. Due to the list to starboard, it proved impossible for the launch of the lifeboats on that side of the ship. The most forward lifeboat on the port side was the captain's motorised launch, but the crew, working along with Second Officer Leonard White, found it difficult to release this boat and they concentrated their efforts on boat numbers 4 and 6 on the port side.

Captain Ferguson had Broadfoot send the following message to *Contest* at 13.21: "Can you see us K." *Contest* replied: "Cannot see you yet." A few minutes later *Contest* again contacted the ship directly: "My ETA now 1415 stop Can you hold out until then K." The destroyer was still 45 minutes from the stricken *Princess Victoria*. There was no way that HMS *Contest* would be able to get to the ship before it sank.

At 13.30 an announcement was made that all passengers should assemble on the weather deck and standby to abandon the ship.

On the deck, crew member Malcolm McKinnon slid down on the starboard side and managed to jump into lifeboat number 5 which was by now in the water. After he released the boat, he then climbed aft and caught hold of the log line which he tied to the ship in an attempt to keep the lifeboat nearby, and hopefully rescue anyone who could get near him. With the force of the waves, the line was carried away and his lifeboat cast adrift.

Passenger David Megarry had climbed up to the deck; all around him were men, women and children holding onto the rails which were by now nearly above their heads. Those that did not have the strength or endurance to hold on had collapsed against the side bulkhead of the lounge. McGarry was standing close to the bridge and heard Captain Ferguson shout to the effect that if the ship had to be abandoned, that everyone was to try and get into the lifeboats or onto a raft. He also said that the destroyer was in the vicinity and searching for them. The captain finished by saying "Good Luck."

Also standing beneath the deck were the Cook John McKnight, luggage man Willie Mann and Bosun William McCarlie. Purser James Morrow, Maynard Sinclair and Steward William Parker were also sitting on the rails and felt that they could clearly see, through a break in the weather, the entrance to Belfast Lough.

As the ship was starting to turn on her side, Mann helped the younger McKnight over the rails onto the side of the ship. The cook was joined by the Bosun McCarlie. McKnight started to make his way along the side of the ship towards the rear, where he could see the lifeboats. After going a few paces, he stopped to look for his ship mate, but McCarlie had been washed away into the sea by the waves.

In the radio room David Broadfoot was by now standing on the side bulkhead of the cabin in order to use the radio equipment, the wall of the cabin now having become the 'floor'. Gallantly he stayed at his post and continued to send and receive messages. In the next few minutes he was to send 15 messages, including several transmissions of the letter 'V' for *Contest* and Portpatrick to try and get a firm bearing on them. At 13.35 he sent:

> SOS Endeavouring to hold on but ship on beam ends can see Irish Coast shall fire rocket if you wish.

A few minutes later Captain Ferguson thought that he could see land and that it was the Copeland Islands; Ferguson had Broadfoot inform Portpatrick of this and at 13.48 he sent the message:

> Captain sez he can see Lighthouse thinks . . . opeltnd [sic] . . . off entrance Belfast Lough Sorry for Morse.

Portpatrick Radio asked if this was Copeland and Broadfoot replied immediately, "Yes." Portpatrick Radio then asked if the ship could get a bearing on the lighthouse, but the reply at 13.48 was:

> Sorry cant see it for squall As As (Wait).

On deck, as the ship was slowly starting to sink deeper into water on the starboard side, many of the passengers tried to pull themselves up and over the port rails. James Carlin, who had earlier pulled his family up to the rails, told them to wait where they were while he went to the stern of the ship to see if any lifeboats were available. He made his way to the stern of the vessel along the sloping deck, but as he got to the stern, the ship began listing more heavily and then started to roll over onto her side. James, who had been holding onto the rails, managed to climb up over them and onto the side of the ship. He then crawled back to where he had left his family, but there was no sign of them. His wife, mother-in-law and sister-in-law had all been washed into the sea. On the sloping deck the two young pantry boys, and second cousins, William McAllister and William Hooper, were clinging on with all their might. Hooper turned to McAllister and told him: "You stay with me and I'll stay with you." A few seconds later Hooper was gone, washed away by the waves.

The crew now started to launch the lifeboats. Ernest Flack, the production manager from Larne, clung to the rails on the port side of the ship and watched with horror as the crew helped the women and children into lifeboat number 4. This boat was then lowered into the water, but when it hit the waves it was driven back against the hull of the ship, broke its back and sank, with all the occupants being thrown into the icy water. The crew, including Chief Officer Duckels, continued in the last few moments to try and launch the other two lifeboats, numbers 2 and 6. Despite the ship starting to turn over on its side, their efforts proved successful in that they managed to get the boats lowered into the water, but due to the 'painter line' still being attached to the ship, the boats were held close to the hull. Able Seamen Garrett, Murdoch, Clements and Nelson managed to get into lifeboat number 6 as it was being lowered down the side.

Somehow Assistant Cook Edward Pritchard with passengers Edmond Freel and Francis Mullan managed to release a second lifeboat from the starboard side and get into it. Sadly, this lifeboat was washed up on the County Down coast with all three men dead.

In the last few minutes before the ship sank another radio message was transmitted at 13.54:

> SOS Estimated position now five miles east of Copelands entrance Belfast Lough.

A couple of seconds later came the message:

> Sorry for morse OM (Old Man) on beam ends.

Attempts had been made to fire rockets, but the first two failed to go off, while the second attempt resulted in them not reaching any great height.

At 13.58 David Broadfoot, the radio operator who had been transmitting messages for over six hours, started to send the very last message that he would ever transmit:

> SOS estimated position now five miles East of Copelands entrance Belfast Lough.

The radio on the *Princess Victoria* now fell silent.

The ship gave a massive lurch and someone shouted, "It's going" and she rolled over onto her side in the water. Those passengers who had not had their grip on the rails wrenched by the violent movement, tried to climb up over them. Many were able to do this on their own, and others with help from fellow passengers and crew. Those who were able to manage this walked along the side of the ship. The two lifeboats that had been launched before the ship went down were now gathered at the stern of the vessel. Passengers and crew who had surmounted the rails and still had strength made their way aft along the side and then the keel, to try to jump into the lifeboats. Billy Copley watched as passenger, and fellow Shorts

worker, Ronnie McNeill climbed over the side rail and jumped into the water. His wife Nan had jumped in just a few minutes before him. Copley recalled that Ronnie swam towards his wife and they both clung onto each other, before they were washed out of view. Albert Dickie had climbed over the rails and onto the side of the ship; he now jumped into the water and swam for a life raft. Maynard Sinclair, after helping Annie Jackson with the children, made his way slowly up to the deck. He told Steward James Blair that he was not just as fit as he used to be, as he had badly injured his leg in the war. Stewardess Mary Close noticed that Sir Walter Smiles had collapsed on the sloping deck; with the help of a steward she managed to get him into a cabin where he was given a glass of water. Sir Walter told her that he had heart trouble and with the water he took a tablet for his condition.

On the deck, Chief Steward Charles Boreland and Steward James Blair bumped into each other. Blair said that hopefully they would get to Larne sometime in the day, but Boreland replied, "Give my friends in Larne my regards, because we have no chance of getting there."

When the *Princess Victoria* sank, the buoyant life rafts that were attached to the rear of the promenade deck broke from their fixings and floated free. These rafts would save several lives. Now in the turbulent cold waters surrounding the ship were three lifeboats, many rafts and a large number of people trying desperately to get to the safety of a boat or raft.

The ship rolled again and turned over onto her back. The upturned hull hung for a few moments, then slowly slid under the waves. The elements had taken their toll, and just a few moments before 14.00, the *Princess Victoria* was gone. For those left in the icy waters the fight for survival had just begun.

**14.00 hours**

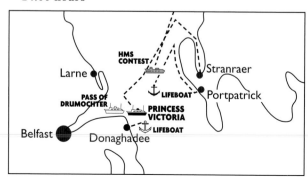

# *The rescue* 7

From the early hours of Saturday morning, when the full effects of the incoming gale had been felt, any ships in the exposed open waters of the Irish Sea had been making a dash for a sheltered haven. Gathered in Belfast Lough waiting for the storm to abate were the *Orchy*, a 1,090-ton general cargo vessel; the *Lairdsmoor*, another general cargo vessel; the *Eastcoates*, a fishing ship; and the 814-ton oil tanker the *Pass of Drumochter*. All of these vessels had for some hours been listening to the distress calls from the *Princess Victoria*. They stayed at anchor in the lough in the belief that the ferry was closer to the Scottish coast and that a tug and a naval destroyer were en route to offer assistance.

At 13.08 James Kelly, captain of the *Pass of Drumochter*, overheard the message from Portpatrick stating that the *Princess Victoria* was stopped and on her beam ends. Kelly contacted Portpatrick and asked for the position of the ship and was given a bearing of 262 degrees from Portpatrick. This bearing, while not reliable, put the ferry on a line about seven miles north of the Copelands. Kelly told Portpatrick that he was about to proceed to their assistance and at 13.25 he had enough steam raised in his ship's boilers to proceed. He was able to set a speed initially of 11½ knots and estimated that he would be in the area within an hour and a half. He then received another message from Portpatrick to say that the *Princess Victoria* could see the Irish coast and could fire rockets. Kelly asked them to do so. As he was passing the *Lairdsmoor*, Kelly alerted her with several short blasts of his whistle. The *Lairdsmoor*, having also had heard the radio messages, raised her anchor and proceeded to help.

At around 14.00 both the *Orchy* and the *Eastcoates* also heard the radio traffic and proceeded to raise steam and proceed to assist. Shortly afterwards these four vessels, along with the Donaghadee lifeboat, were proceeding as quickly as they could to try to locate the *Princess Victoria* and her passengers and crew.

Only a few miles to the east of these ships, a desperate battle for survival was being fought in the icy cold waters of the Irish Sea. When the ship overturned and sank, only those passengers who could hang on to the rails and climb over them now stood any chance of surviving. With the sea temperature at around 4° C, there would be little chance of surviving long in the water.

Scattered around were now only four of the ship's lifeboats and several rafts. Lifeboat number 4, which had been full of women and children, had smashed against the hull and sank, with all the occupants being thrown into the water. James Kerr, the captain of one of Kelly's coal boats, had managed to get into lifeboat number 6. This was the boat that was to save most of those who were to survive. As the ship was sinking, people were jumping into the boat while several others, including Able Seamen Alec Craig and Albert Dickie, were pulled from the water into the safety of its confines. James Carlin, who had just lost his whole family when they were washed away from beside him, was another man who jumped into boat number 6, breaking his ribs as he tumbled down. It was only as the boat was filling up with men that it was noticed that the painter line was still attached to the sinking ship. If this line was not quickly severed the lifeboat would be dragged under by *Princess Victoria* as she plummeted to the bottom of the Irish Sea. James Kerr moved forward in the boat, pulled out his pen knife and cut the line.

An artist's impression of the last moments before the sinking of the *Princess Victoria*. Scattered around in the sea are only three lifeboats.
*BBC Northern Ireland*

In the freezing waters the gale was still blowing with gusts at around 40 to 60 knots, generating waves up to nine metres in height.

All of the lifeboats had their oars washed away with the impact of entering the water. This meant that the survivors in the boats were not able to row to the others in the water; rather, those in the water had to try and swim to the boats or the rafts. Fusilier Geoffrey Bingley, who was in boat number 6, saw a woman on a raft but they were unable to get near her and she was washed into the sea.

Ernest Flack, who had jumped into this boat from the upturned hull, looked around and saw many women on rafts, including Wrens Violet Dingle and Eileen Prentice who were both washed off by the large waves. David Megarry swam to one of the lifeboats and grabbed onto one of the lifelines. He held on for about 15 minutes with another man hanging on beside him. After a short period of time, this other man's strength and determination left him and he dropped off the line into the icy water. McGarry was then able to get his leg up onto the boat and was hauled in.

An artist's impression of hauling the lucky few on board one of the lifeboats.                    *BBC Northern Ireland*

Steward James Blair had jumped onto a life raft and had witnessed the lifeboat that was full of women and children being smashed against the hull of the ship. He started to paddle in the water to try and get closer to lifeboat number 6. Blair then jumped for the lifeboat and managed to grab onto the side, from where he was hauled into it. As he looked into the water he saw the bodies of the two Mooney children, whom he had earlier helped into their life jackets.

Pulling in the last few survivors.          *BBC Northern Ireland*

In lifeboat number 2, Kenneth Rotherham had grasped the side of the boat as it was being lowered just before the ship sank. He had to cut the line connecting the boat to the ship and allow the boat to drift away. Ivor Thomas, who had earlier rescued some passengers by pulling them through the lounge window, was now swimming for his life in the cold waters. He made it to boat 6 and was pulled in, but in the process lost his trousers and spent some time lying in the bottom of the boat to try and keep warm.

Those who could not reach the lifeboats swam to the rafts that were scattered about. James Gilmore got into lifeboat number 6, but was concerned that the painter line wasn't being cut quickly enough and thought that the boat would be dragged down with the ship. He jumped into the water and managed to get onto a life raft. James later described the sight around him as terrible, with a lot of bodies floating about in the water; many passengers had jumped into the water with their life jackets on and the impact seemed to have knocked them out. A wave then turned Gilmore's raft over and tossed him into the sea, but he managed to hang onto the line dangling from the life raft.

Nearby, John Fitzpatrick had also clambered onto a raft and was joined by a young lady who told him her name was Lilly Russell and that she was travelling to Donegal to visit her sick mother. The raft was then hit by a wave and Lilly Russell was washed off; Fitzpatrick could do nothing to save her.

Joseph Hastings, and the other men who were in lifeboat number 2, had just witnessed the lifeboat full of women and children break up against the hull and now

Clinging on for dear life in the face of 40-foot waves.

*BBC Northern Ireland*

An empty life raft bears a silent witness to the terrible disaster.

*Belfast Telegraph*

saw a lady from that lifeboat in the water close to them. She was wearing a heavy fur coat and as the men were unable to manoeuvre the boat, they called for her to try to swim towards them. Hastings recalled that the lady's coat seemed to be dragging her down, and the men shouted at her to try and take the coat off. As she started to do this, clearly visible under the coat were several bags of money. The unknown lady was overcome by exhaustion and the waves and was washed away from them.

William Copley had dived into the water from the keel of the upturned ferry, after witnessing people jump into the water and being crushed between a lifeboat and the hull. Along with Billy McClenaghan, he swam towards a raft and hauled himself up onto it by using the attached lifeline. The raft was carried away from McClenaghan and Copley could do nothing to help him. This raft also had two men and one woman on it. After about 30 minutes the woman's strength left her and she slid into the water and disappeared. One of the men on the raft was William Carter, who was steward on the *Princess Margaret*. Copley later recalled that when they were on the raft the sea conditions were horrendous, with mountainous waves of over 30 feet in height crashing down on them. He remembers clearly how William Carter stood up on the middle of the raft and started singing 'The Lord's My Shepherd'. After he had finished singing, Carter pointed into the distance and said, "There is a ship." Copley recalled Carter then walked off the raft and into the sea.

Of the *Princess Victoria*'s 'human cargo' only 44

survived in three lifeboats and six life rafts, being buffeted and tossed around in the continuing gale that gave no sign of abating. Scattered around them were the bodies of many of their fellow passengers and crew. In one of the lifeboats the survivors tried to paddle with their hands to get near those still alive in the water, but their attempts at navigating the small craft were no match for the weather. The lifeboats were supposed to carry two axes, some biscuits, two tins of distress rockets, sail, mast, oars, condensed milk, chocolate and a sea anchor, but everything had been washed out of the boats except the sea anchor and the flares. In boat number 6, which held over 30 survivors, James Kelly the sea captain took charge. Kelly had the sea anchor deployed, a device designed to keep the boat facing into the weather. He also organised letting off some of the distress flares. Lifeboat number 4 held six survivors, while Malcolm McKinnon was the sole occupant in boat number 5; seven other men were clinging on for dear life to rafts in the water.

In Portpatrick Coastguard station, District Controller

William Spreadborough was coordinating the rescue. Prestwick Airport was contacted to enquire if an aeroplane could be made available to assist with the search for the ship. Prestwick Air Traffic Control contacted the RAF who quickly made radio contact with an aeroplane that had just left Prestwick and asked it to divert to the Copeland Islands, which it did. A Hastings aircraft, with Captain Henry Owen in charge, which had been en route to the Butt of Lewis to search for the trawler *Michael Griffith*, was also diverted to the Copelands. The Coastguard had also been in contact with the British Railways office at Stranraer, where the Clerk John Maxwell had contacted Murrays, the local bus company, to arrange from them to have buses patrolling the shoreline from Corsewall Point to Stranraer in case any survivors came ashore. Maxwell also arranged with local hotels to be ready with food and beds if needed.

In Portpatrick Radio station, Operator William Ross, who had taken in Morse code the first distress message from the *Princess Victoria*, was now working the radio that was in voice contact with the rescue ships. At 14.49, 51 minutes after the last message from David Broadfoot on the *Princess Victoria*, the radio burst into life with a message from Captain Hugh Matheson of the *Orchy*:

Have come across oil and wreckage and life jackets approximately five miles east of Mew Island.

A minute later the *Orchy* was informing Portpatrick Radio that they could see people on rafts waving at them.

High overhead, Captain Owen in the Hastings aircraft was approaching the same scene and radioed that he too could see wreckage and oil in the water. As the weather had by now closed in and visibility was limited, Owen was forced to fly his plane under the cloud and at times was no more than 100 feet above sea level. While passing over the area, the aeroplane dropped Lindholme emergency gear. This rescue equipment consisted of five cylinders, one containing a dingy which inflates on contact with water and the other four containing waterproof suits, water, emergency rations, distress flares and chemical bags to generate heat on contact with the water. This equipment was dropped near rafts which held survivors, the plane also dropping markers for the rescue vessels to see and home onto.

Portpatrick Radio then broadcast a message to all shipping in the vicinity, appealing for them to make for the position of the *Orchy* to assist in the rescue of the survivors.

While Matheson was waiting for the other rescue vessels to join him, he had his crew put ropes, rope ladders and lifebuoys with lines attached over the side of his ship, to help get the people out of the water. With the ship rolling and pitching heavily, those in the water could not get hold of the ropes as they were exhausted. Matheson said that there were women in the water who

Lifeboat number 6, holding the majority of survivors, lies dangerously close to the stern of the oil tanker the *Pass of Drumochter*.
*Belfast Telegraph*

were dead. The *Orchy* was unable to launch any of her lifeboats, as the height of the waves was so great that her captain feared they would have smashed before reaching the water. Matheson recalled that the weather throughout this most tricky and precarious operation was very severe, with heavy seas squalls of sleet and the wind blowing at hurricane force.

At about 15.00, and now just over an hour after the last message from the ship, the *Pass of Drumochter* was the first vessel to rendezvous with the *Orchy*. Captain James Kelly was the master of the tanker and when he sighted a lifeboat, which was number 6 and full of survivors, he circled round the boat and made a line fast. However, owing to the weather the lifeboat got under the stern quarter and was in danger of being sunk. In an attempt to rescue the people in the lifeboat, the crew of the oil tanker threw a Jacob's ladder over the side of their ship to see if anyone could climb to safety. Chief Cook of the *Princess Victoria*, John McKnight, tried to climb up the ladder from the lifeboat to the tanker, but as he put his weight on the ladder, it gave way – the crew of the oil tanker had not tied it off tightly to the deck of the ship. McKnight fell off the ladder into the sea and got his hand caught in one of the gunwales of the lifeboat, subsequently suffering a serious injury. As he fell backwards into the sea, McKnight managed to grasp hold of one of the lifelines attached to the side of the lifeboat. Those still in the lifeboat thought that he had been washed away, but the crew of the tanker spotted him and yelled down to the lifeboat to haul him in, which they did. The *Pass of Drumochter* was rising and falling with the

Lifeboat number 6 with the sea anchor deployed awaiting rescue.                                              *Planet News*

waves and with every rise the lifeboat was being drawn close in to the exposed propellers. As the ship fell back off the wave the lifeboat was being pushed back into the water. The survivors were in a desperate situation. Either the tanker would have to move away from them or the lifeboat would be drawn under her stern and be smashed by the exposed propellers.

Sensing that the lifeboat was in danger of being overwhelmed by the sea and conscious of the threat posed by the close proximity of the tanker, Captain Kelly called up the Donaghadee lifeboat by radio and asked them to come and try to take these survivors on board. Gingerly,

The *Sir Samuel Kelly*, the lifeboat based at Donaghadee.
                                              *Q Nelson collection*

Coxswain Hugh Nelson manoeuvred the *Sir Samuel Kelly* closer and closer to the small boat in the water. He finally managed to get along side it and all passengers were now transferred to the safety of the lifeboat and the warmth that her cabin offered. No sooner had Nelson and his crew finished this rescue, when he was called up again by Kelly on the *Pass of Drumochter* to say that he had seen another lifeboat, with only one man in it. Kelly suggested to Nelson that he would move to the wind side of this lifeboat and set up some shelter for it while the lifeboat could edge towards it. This tricky manoeuvre was slowly accomplished and the sole occupant in boat number 5 – Malcolm McKinnon – was also taken on board the *Sir Samuel Kelly*. The Donaghadee lifeboat proceeded on and came across John Fitzpatrick clinging for all he was worth to a life-raft. Hugh Nelson junior, a member of the lifeboat crew, recalled that due to the excess cold Fitzpatrick's arms were practically locked onto the raft. They slowly inched up to the raft and took the exhausted Fitzpatrick on board.

HMS *Contest* had been in the area for about 30 minutes when they saw a lifeboat with six men in it. With the swell in the sea the lifeboat was being lifted up to nearly the height of the deck of the destroyer. The naval crew were able to pull all six men off the boat. Shortly afterwards they came across two men on separate rafts. John Murray had managed to remain on top of one the rafts, while on the other one, James Gilmore was hanging on. Both these men were nearly at the end of their endurance, having spent well over an hour in the freezing water. Getting them on board, with the heavy rolling seas and the danger of them being sucked under the ship, was to prove very difficult.

Captain Fleming instructed two officers on the ship, Lieutenant SL McArdle and Chief Boatswain's Mate Wilfred Warren to go over the side into the water and effect the rescue. McArdle nearly disappeared under the ship, as he hit the bilge keel with his shoulder on the way back to the surface following his dive in, and he had to be rescued as well. Boatswain's Mate Wilfred Warren managed to get a line around each man and they were pulled up to the safety of the ship. James Gilmore recalls that when he was 'landed' on the deck, the crew dragged him to the boiler room to warm up. He had been wearing a very heavy overcoat known as a Crombie, and this had probably saved his life, keeping at least a little warmth in his body during the long exposure to the cold water.

On the bridge of *Contest*, Fleming informed his headquarters of his actions and was given permission to proceed to Belfast to take the survivors to safety.

Lieutenant Commander Harry Fleming, captain of HMS *Contest*.
*Larne Times*

Petty Officer Wilfred Warren who dived from HMS *Contest* into the Irish Sea to assist survivors.
*County Down Spectator*

Meanwhile, David Brewster, the skipper of the trawler *Eastcoates*, was coming among survivors in the water. With the very heavy waves he also was unable to launch his boats. He was able to get his trawler close to the people in the water, only to have a large wave come up and sweep them out of reach. His crew were on deck with long poles trying to reach those nearby. By this stage the visibility was about half a mile.

They eventually managed to get seven people on board, six of whom were dead. Two of the dead were in uniform and were possibly crew, while the remaining four bodies were those of women. The man who was hauled alive from a raft was Petty Officer Beer, who was semi-conscious. On checking the bodies, Brewster later stated that the life jackets were hard up under their chins, giving him the impression that they had choked when they jumped overboard.

The Portpatrick lifeboat had been in the area since around 15.00 and came across two rafts, each with one male survivor on board. They rescued Billy Copley and John Yeomans, while continuing to search for any more survivors until dark

The Donaghadee lifeboat, the *Sir Samuel Kelly*, with 33 survivors now secure in her cabins and engine room, left the rescue area and made for Donaghadee. En route the crew handed the survivors cigarettes. Albert Dickie remembers that one of the crew produced a bottle of rum, which was passed around. He recalled the warming effect of the spirit: "By God it was good." The lifeboat finally arrived at Donaghadee harbour at around 18.00 and disembarked the survivors.

Word of the disaster had been broadcast on the radio and many people were standing by at the County Down town to assist those that had been through so much, in any way possible. The Imperial, a local hotel on the promenade, owned by Angus and Hazel Campbell, was made ready to receive the passengers of the *Princess Victoria*. Out at sea the Portpatrick lifeboat started to make her way to Donaghadee with her two survivors, arriving in the safety of the harbour at around 19.15. HMS *Contest*, which was still searching for any survivors off the Copeland Islands, was joined at around 19.50 by HMS *Woodbridge Haven*, a Royal Navy frigate commanded by Lieutenant Commander Brian Cochrane. The *Woodbridge Haven* now assumed tactical command.

**Left:** The crew of the Donaghadee lifeboat *Sir Samuel Kelly*.
L–R: Samuel Herron, John Trimble, Samuel Nelson, James Armstrong, Coxswain Hugh Nelson (seated), Alec Nelson, Hugh Nelson Jnr, George Lindsay, William Nelson, Frank Nelson.
*County Down Spectator*

**Below:** Some of the survivors being landed at Donaghadee harbour following their terrible ordeal.
*County Down Spectator*

The two navy ships began a further search of an area of 32 square miles to the south of the last known position of the *Princess Victoria*. *Contest*, with her eight survivors, broke off from the search at about 22.00 hours and made for Belfast harbour, finally docking and discharging the survivors at around 23.30.

The trawler *Eastcoates* had radioed Portpatrick Radio to tell them that their captain was unsure of the entrance to Belfast and asked if it would be possible for the survivor John Beer, whom they had rescued, to be transferred to another vessel. The Donaghadee lifeboat was contacted as she lay docked at Donaghadee and once more went to sea to rendezvous with the *Eastcoates* at Briggs Buoy in Belfast Lough, near Whitehead. As the lifeboat approached the trawler, the sea was too rough to transfer Beer, so both vessels moved to smoother waters, where the transfer of six bodies (four women and two men), survivor John Beer and seven bags of mail took place. The lifeboat arrived back in Donaghadee at about 01.30 on 1 February. John Beer, finally after 18 hours, had made the crossing from Scotland to Northern Ireland and was the last survivor to be brought ashore.

At first light the following morning, Sunday, the search

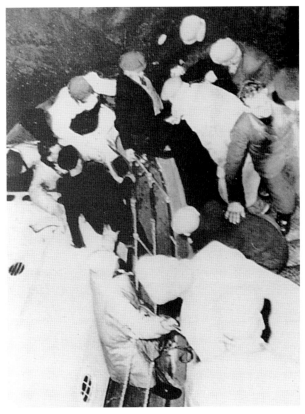

HMS *Woodbridge Haven* – on her arrival the ship assumed
tactical command of the search area.          *Royal Navy*

for survivors began again. HMS *Contest* sailed from
Belfast at around 05.00 and rejoined the *Woodbridge
Haven* which had stayed at sea all night. They were joined
by a third naval frigate, the *Launceston Castle*, at 07.30
at Mew Island. A zigzag search was carried out to the
south of the Islands. A number of bodies were sighted
and *Contest* stopped to effect recovery. A total of 17
bodies, including those of Captain James Ferguson, Sir
Walter Smiles and Maynard Sinclair, were recovered. The
search south carried on until 13.30 with the naval ships
returning to Mew Island and recovering more bodies. By
dark, *Contest* had recovered 32 bodies and the
*Woodbridge Haven* 12 bodies. Both proceeded to Belfast
and docked at 19.30. The bodies were then handed over
to the authorities. *Contest* finally sailed from Belfast in
the afternoon of Monday, 2 February.

The Donaghadee lifeboat went to sea at 07.00 on the
Sunday morning and proceeded to search in a southerly
direction. The weather was fine, with the sea a flat calm,
such a difference from the previous 24 hours. During the
day they sighted wreckage and took on board the bodies
of 11 males, one female and one child. They also
recovered three bags of mail.

Hugh Nelson, the 20-year-old son of the lifeboat's
coxswain, still clearly remembers being told by his father
to lie on the deck of the lifeboat, with another crew
member, and lean over the side to haul on board the
bodies whose clothes the other crew members had snared
with boat hooks. For almost 12 hours the crew of the *Sir
Samuel Kelly* was engaged in this search until they
eventually returned to Donaghadee at 7.15 pm.

Once the news of the loss of the ship had become
known in Donaghadee, a large number of people
travelled to the harbour, anxiously awaiting any news of
survivors. Angus and Hazel Campbell, who had since

1939 owned the Imperial Hotel in the town, were in their
home in Belfast when they heard the news on the radio.
They immediately made their way to Donaghadee to see
if they could offer any assistance. When they arrived at
the hotel, which was situated on the parade in the town,
overlooking the harbour, they at first had trouble getting
in, due to the number of people who had gathered
awaiting news. Once in the hotel, along with Miss
Semple, their manageress, they set about arranging beds,
bedding, towels and hot water bottles as well as having
the kitchen staff prepare hot soup and food for all those
involved. The dining room was set up as a morgue, to
receive any bodies that would be brought ashore.

While Angus Campbell organised the hotel and the staff,
his wife Hazel manned the telephone, answering many
calls from people seeking any new piece of information.
She recalled that one reporter for the *Belfast News Letter*
practically monopolised the telephone, filing her report to
the paper. Eventually when the telephone was
overwhelmed with calls, Mrs Campbell arranged for the
local police to answer the incoming calls.

Local members of the British Red Cross made their
way to the hotel where Miss McNarry, the local
commandant, and Mrs Gordon Campbell, the honorary
secretary, busied themselves with preparations to receive
any survivors from the stricken ship. They were joined by
Mrs HP Gilbert OBE, the county director of the British
Red Cross. Mrs Gilbert was also a director of Welfare
Services in Northern Ireland, and had travelled recently
on the *Princess Victoria*. A fleet of ambulances was
assembled and the local Salvation Army brought clothing
to the hotel. The Royal Ulster Constabulary also
dispatched officers to assist in compiling a list of those
who had survived.

Mrs Eileen Gilbert, county
director of the British Red Cross,
who organised comfort and
assistance for the survivors at
Donaghadee.

*County Down Spectator*

One survivor, William Copley, recalled that when he was landed at the harbour at Donaghadee he was taken to the Imperial Hotel. By the time he arrived he was freezing and one of the first people he met was Mr Thomas Clokey, who on seeing the state of Copley, produced a bottle of Black Bush whiskey and asked the near frozen Copley if he wanted a drop to warm him up. The 'medicine' was quickly taken. Afterwards Copley, who was still fully clothed, was placed into a hot bath to warm him up. When he was a bit warmer he managed to get a change of clothing. An ambulance was leaving the hotel bound for Belfast and Copley secured a lift home. An overjoyed wife received him safely home and put him straight to bed. Copley recalls:

> I was just into bed when an Official from the Ulster Transport Authority called at the house to tell my wife that I was safe, in Donaghadee. She replied "No he is not." The Official then repeated the fact that I was safe and well in Donaghadee, to which my wife replied, "He is upstairs in bed."

Shortly after this a doctor arrived at the house and Copley remembers receiving a telling-off for leaving the hotel at Donaghadee before having a medical. Following an examination he was given a clean bill of health.

Three days later, Angus and Hazel Campbell received a personal letter from Sir Basil Brookeborough, the Prime Minister of Northern Ireland. In the letter the Prime Minister thanked the Campbells for the help they had given to the survivors:

> I feel sure that you have received many sincere expressions of thanks from those most closely concerned for the great kindness you showed to so many of the survivors from the terrible tragedy which overtook the Princess Victoria. I should like however to add to them those of myself and my colleagues in the Government. To throw open your hotel to those who had not to be taken to hospital, and to enable them to receive first-aid, comfort and attention, after their awful ordeal was an act of real Christian charity and I am sure it will long be remembered by the recipients with deepest gratitude.

Yours sincerely

Brookeborough

In the early hours of Sunday morning, William McAllister, Kenneth Harrison, James Blair, John Stanford, Thomas Curry and Ivor Thomas, all of whom had originally been taken to the Imperial Hotel, were transported to the nearby Bangor Hospital. Here they were given a full medical examination, had a hot bath and were allowed to rest, under the watchful eye of the hospital's matron, Miss SL Currie. By the afternoon all seven had been discharged. John McKnight, the ship's cook, was transferred to Newtownards Hospital, where he was to spend nearly six weeks recovering from the injury to his hand and fingers sustained while trying to climb from the lifeboat into the *Pass of Drumochter*.

With all the survivors that were to be rescued now being cared for by the authorities or safely home with loved ones, attention turned to the identification of the bodies that had been picked up.

The remains that had been recovered from the Irish Sea were taken to various locations to await official identification. In Belfast, morgues were set up at the City Hospital, the Royal Victoria Hospital and the Belfast City Morgue. Another morgue was set up at Newtownards Hospital. Members of the Royal Ulster Constabulary and hospital officials had the unpleasant task of trying to identify the recovered bodies by their possessions. Where this was not possible, the body was stripped and covered in white cloth, while possessions and valuables were collected and placed beside the body to await identification by relatives.

Many of the relatives lived outside Belfast and one of the problems they encountered was travelling to the various locations to search for loved ones. In 1953, car ownership was not as widespread as today and many of the distressed relatives did not own any form of vehicle. Great reliance was placed on the generosity of friends and neighbours to provide transport. In fact, many of the bodies were identified by friends, prior to their being released for burial.

Some of the relatives had a longer wait before the remains of their loved ones could be released, as not all of the bodies were washed up near Belfast or Donaghadee. A total of eight bodies were recovered at the Isle of Man and Inquests were held there, prior to the remains being released. Off Londonderry a further three bodies were recovered, while two more were recovered at Luce Bay and Whithorn Bay in Scotland.

Eventually 100 bodies were recovered, including that of three-year-old Stephen Childs.

# The human cargo

During the Inquiry into the loss of the *Princess Victoria*, the chairman, Mr JH Campbell QC RM, stated that perhaps the true figure of the number of people lost would never be fully known. In his final Report, question 43 asked, "How many lives were lost" and the answer given was, "According to information supplied by the Ministry of Transport 133 lives were lost."

Only ten male crew members and 34 male passengers survived. All the women, children and senior officers on board the ship were lost. Adding this figure of 44 to the figures for those lost, as supplied by the Ministry, gives a total compliment of 177 who departed with the ship on that Saturday morning.

Mr Campbell also stated in the Report that there were 49 crew members on board the ship when it left Stranraer on 31 January 1953. In researching the crew and passengers who travelled, there was one major problem that I encountered. None of the records that would have been assembled after the loss of the ship, of the names of survivors or those lost, and held by the various public bodies, are available today. To further compound this lack of information, British Railways were not required to maintain a manifest of their passengers. Today it is a legal requirement that shipping companies do maintain this type of record.

The *Princess Margaret*, the sister ship of the *Princess Victoria*, had been dry docked in north Wales with her crew having been discharged for the period of the ongoing work. Some of these crew members made their way to Stranraer and travelled to Larne on the last voyage of the

*Princess Victoria*. This gives rise to further confusion as to who actually comprised the crew on the day, as various reports in newspapers assumed that the crew of the *Princess Margaret* was in fact the crew of the *Princess Victoria*. In Appendix 2, I have listed the crew that I believe was in charge of the ship for this, her last, voyage.

In my research I have drawn from various sources to try to compile a full and definitive list of the people who travelled on the *Princess Victoria*. Information has been taken from various sources, including newspaper reports of the period, statements from survivors, interviews with survivors, and comments relating to individuals made during the formal Inquiry. I have, as with my previous book *Titanic Belfast's Own*, been only too aware of the need to be completely certain of my facts before adding to the list of names. Following extensive research, I have found that there was one extra person who travelled on the ship. This number is above the official figure given in the Inquiry, but it is my firm belief that this person did in fact travel on the *Princess Victoria* and therefore should be included in the list of names.

In this chapter I wish to make mention of each person that sailed on the *Princess Victoria*. It is an important part of the story of the vessel that those who were lost and those who survived are not forgotten. I have spent many months researching the lives of these people and I would like to thank the relatives of those who embarked at Stranraer on the *Princess Victoria* for allowing me to invade their privacy and for all the help and assistance that they gave me over my period of investigation.

# Crew of the Princess Victoria

### Robert Campbell Ball (L)

Robert, who was aged 25, was the fifth engineer serving on the ship. He lived at Windsor Road, Belfast. He had been married for just over three years and had a young daughter. He served with the RAF during the closing years of World War Two. Following service in the merchant navy and on shore as a motor mechanic, he joined the crew of the *Princess Victoria* in order to be based nearer his home and family in Belfast.

### Roseann Baxter (L)

Roseann, aged 39, was a stewardess from Larne, whose address was 11 Gardenmore Park. She was the eldest in a family of five boys and two girls. She had previously worked as a weaver and as a shop assistant. Her pastimes included dancing and she had won first prize for the fox-trot at a competition held in the Victoria Hall in Larne. When World War Two started she joined the Wrens and then had a job with the Ministry of Food during the final period of food rationing. In 1950 she joined the cross-channel service, initially on the *Princess Margaret* and then transferred to the *Princess Victoria*. She was last seen on the deck of the ship holding a baby in her arms.

### James Blair (S)

James Blair, who was aged 42, lived at Salisbury Terrace in Larne and was a steward on the *Princess Victoria*. He had been at sea since 1928 and had been on the ship for four to five years. When the vessel was hit by the first heavy sea, Blair was in the smoke room and had helped

passengers who had been thrown out of their seats. Later he handed out life jackets. He was friendly with Captain Ferguson, who at one stage told him that tugs and a destroyer were coming to assist them. He made his escape from the ship in lifeboat number 6, walking off the hull straight into the lifeboat without even getting his feet wet. Following the loss, James did not go back to the cross-channel route, but decided to go to work on the deep sea instead. He retired from the sea at age 65 and died in 1992.

### William C Blair (L)

William Blair had been a steward on the *Princess Margaret* and lived at Glynnview Avenue, Larne. He was 33 years old and was married with one son. Prior to World War Two he lived and worked in Bournemouth. William served in the army during the war and after demobilisation returned to Larne to start working on the cross-channel ferries.

### J Charles Boreland (L)

Charles Boreland was the chief steward on the *Princess Victoria*. He had served on the Larne crossing for over 30 years. Charles originally came from Glasgow, and was wounded in World War One while serving in the Royal Welsh

Fusiliers. He served on the *Princess Margaret* which was bombed during the evacuation of troops from Dunkirk in 1940.

### Hugh Brennan (L)

Hugh, who was in his mid-forties, was married and a native of Larne, living at Crescent Gardens. He was on the crew of the *Princess Margaret* but was transferred to the *Princess Victoria* in the role of purser. He was a brother-in-law of Douglas Murray who was a greaser on the ship. Hugh had served on the 1939 *Princess Victoria* which was sunk in the Humber in World War Two. He was described as a perfect gentleman who went out of his way in his role of purser to help and assist passengers. He was last seen on the deck of the ship helping children into one of the lifeboats. A very talented woodworker, Hugh made furniture and violins.

### David Broadfoot (L)

David Broadfoot, who was aged 53, was married with a teenage son and lived at Royal Crescent, Stranraer. He had been at sea since 1915. Normally he was the radio operator on the *Princess Margaret*, but was on relief duty for this voyage. As the radio operator on the *Princess Victoria*, he was hailed as a hero for the way he stayed at his post, transmitting until practically the end. David was even to apologise for the standard of his Morse during his last transmissions. Following the loss, he was posthumously awarded the George Cross, presented to his wife and son by Queen Elizabeth II. The medal was recently presented by Broadfoot's son to the Stranraer Museum.

### John Campbell (L)

John lived at Ailsa Crescent in Stranraer. He had been an able seaman on the crew of the ship since 1947. Prior to that date, he had worked in the grocery trade.

### Catherine Clark (L)

Catherine, a bureau assistant on the *Princess Victoria*, lived at Arran Road in Gourock. She was the longest-serving female member of crew on the Princess class ships. Catherine was very friendly with Margaret McKnight, wife of the *Princess Victoria*'s cook, John McKnight.

### Mary D Close (L)

Mary, who lived at Bay Park, Larne, was a bureau assistant on the ship. She was seen helping the children off the ship into one of the lifeboats. That lifeboat was subsequently lost with all on board.

### Alexander WB Craig (S)

Alec had been at sea since 1947 and had been an able seaman on the ship for the previous 18 months. He lived at West End Terrace, Stranraer. After the sea breached the rear stern doors, he had a rope tied around him and, armed with a crowbar, had tried unsuccessfully to close the doors. Later he tried to launch the captain's motor lifeboat, but again without success. Alec was thrown into the water as the ship keeled over, having then to swim to the safety of lifeboat number 6.

### Shirley Duckels (L)

Shirley was the chief officer on the *Princess Victoria*. In the absence of the captain, he would assume the latter's duties. He was married and lived at Bowling Green Road, Stranraer, having just recently moved house. Shirley joined the service in 1935 and was originally from Goole. He was well liked by all who knew him and was considered to be a very capable and confident officer.

### James M Ferguson (L)

James Millar Ferguson was the master of the *Princess Victoria*. He lived at Stranraer with his wife and two children. He served his apprenticeship at sea with the Allen Line and was given a commission in the Royal Engineers in World War One. Following the war he was appointed second officer on the Larne to Stranraer route. In 1936 he was given his first command on the *Princess Margaret*. He also was captain of the *Princess Maud* for three years. In World War Two Ferguson commanded the *Princess Margaret*, taking part in the D-Day operations. He was appointed captain of the *Princess Victoria* when the ship was commissioned in 1947.

### Edmond Freel (L)

Edmond, who was aged 29 years, was the fourth engineer on the ship. He lived at Ashbrook Crescent, Belfast, and was married with a young son and daughter. He had originally worked at the Harland and Wolff shipyard in Belfast and after World War Two had joined the merchant navy, travelling widely. Edmond had decided to leave the employment of British Railways and

return to the Belfast shipyards. To get some extra money to purchase tools, he was working an additional weekend shift prior to leaving the *Princess Victoria*. His body was recovered from a lifeboat that was washed up at Kearney Point on the County Down coast.

### John Garrett (S)

John, an able seaman on the ship, lived at Agnew Crescent in Stranraer. He assisted with the attempt to close the rear stern doors when they burst open. He also tried to clear the scuppers on the car deck to allow the water to flow away. Due to the shift in the cargo, John was unable to get near them. He left the ship in lifeboat number 6.

### William Gowan (L)

William was the carpenter on the *Princess Victoria*. He was 26 years of age and came from Portavogie. He was married and had a four-week-old son called Billy. William trained as a carpenter at Harland and Wolff in Belfast and went to sea in 1946 after completing his apprenticeship. In 1951 he had been shipwrecked when the *Paris City* broke her back off the coast of Spain. He was due to finish his time at sea in February 1953 and had planned to restart employment with Harland and Wolff.

### William Hardie (L)

William was the quartermaster on the ship. He was married with a grown-up family and came from Broomfield Gardens in Stranraer. He had joined the cross-channel service in 1920.

### William Hooper (L)

William was a pantry boy on the ship. He was aged 17 and lived at Bank Road, Larne, with his parents and six brothers and sisters. His older brothers were at sea and his dream was to follow them, repeatedly seeking his parents' permission. He had worked on the Larne to Stranraer route for the previous 11 months and had just been transferred from the *Princess Margaret* four weeks prior to the loss. At the weekend the family home would be full of crew from the *Princess Victoria*, as Billy would bring them home to 'sleep over' for the night. Two of his brothers had previously served on the *Princess Victoria*. On hearing the news of the disaster, his mother collapsed. His father and elder brother had to travel to Belfast to identify his body. William was a second cousin of William McAllister, the other pantry boy on the ship.

### Wesley Kerr (L)

Wesley, a steward on the ship, lived at Fleet Street in Larne. He was aged 25 and was married with a young daughter. He had previously been a company rep, and had only joined the ship as a stopgap a few weeks before the sinking. He had another job which he hoped to start within a few days. Wesley was described as a very pleasant man who would have gone out of his way to help anyone.

### Fergie Leckie (L)

Fergie, who lived at Sun Street, Stranraer, was one of the quartermasters on the ship. He had originally been

a fisherman and had joined the cross-channel service in 1948. His body was washed up at Castletown on the Isle of Man a few days after the sinking.

### Horace Locke (L)

Horace, a native of Stranraer, was a married man who lived in Albert Street in Larne. He was the pantry man on the ship, having previously worked for many years on the *Princess Margaret* before being transferred to the *Princess Victoria*. He was not due to sail on the ship on 31 January, but stood in for a crewmate who was attending a wedding. He and his wife, Agnes, had a boy and a girl and his wife was expecting their third child when the ship was lost. For many years he had worked in the Auld Kings Arms Hotel in Stranraer.

### Alexander McAllister (L)

Alex lived at John Simpson Drive, Stranraer, and was a greaser on the ship. He had been at sea since 1918 and was married with a grown-up family.

### William McAllister (S)

William was aged 17. He was a pantry boy in the ship's galley. As the *Princess Victoria* was sinking he jumped into lifeboat number 6. He was the second cousin of William Hooper, the other pantry boy on board.

### William McCarlie (L)

William, who was married, was the bosun on the ship and lived at Dalrymole Street in Stranraer. He was one of the oldest members of the crew, due to retire within a few months. He served on the cross-channel steamers during World War One.

### James McCowan (L)

James, who was aged 50, was a second steward on the ship. He was a married man who lived at McDowall Drive, Stranraer. His brother was chief steward on the *Princess Margaret* and another brother was also at sea. James had joined the cross-channel service in 1937.

### William McGarel (L)

William, who was aged 55, was a quartermaster on the ship. He had served in the army and fought at the Battle of the Somme in World War One. He lived at Glynn Road, Larne, with his wife and their three boys and two girls.

### William McInnes (L)

William was the second engineer on the ship. He came originally from the Clyde region but moved to Stranraer in 1942 when he joined the crew of the *Princess Maud*, before being transferred to the *Princess Victoria*. William was married with a young family.

### Malcolm McKinnon (S)

Malcolm was an able seaman who lived at Castle Kennedy, Wigtownshire. He had been at sea since 1938 and had served on the *Princess*

*Victoria* for four and a half years. He was part of the unsuccessful attempt to release the bow rudder of the ship. As the ship was starting to go over on its side, he slid down and fell into lifeboat number 5. The boat had no oars in it and he was unable to recuse any survivors in the water or to stay near the sinking ship. He was picked up by the Donaghadee lifeboat.

### John McKnight (S)

John, who was the chief cook on the ship, had just returned to duty on the previous Thursday following his honeymoon. He had previously seen active service in World War Two as one of the Desert Rats. He was aged 32 and had been a cook for four years. As the ship was sinking he jumped into a lifeboat and was rescued by the Donaghadee lifeboat.

### David McMillan (L)

David was aged 21 and had just completed his national service with the Royal Scots Fusiliers in Germany. He joined the ship in June and was appointed as pantryman. David lived at John Simpson Drive, Stranraer.

### Thomas B McQuiston (S)

Thomas was from Mount Vernon Road, Stranraer, and was a cargoman on the ship. He had served on the *Princess Victoria* since she first entered service. Thomas was part of the group that tried to close the rear stern doors. As the ship was sinking he slid down the hull and got into lifeboat number 6. This boat hit the hull of the ship but managed to stay afloat and he was picked up by the Donaghadee lifeboat.

### William Mann (L)

William was aged 59 and was the luggage man on the ship. He lived at Coastguard Road in Larne and was married with a grown-up daughter. He had worked on the cross-channel ferries for many years and had previously been bosun. When he suffered the loss of a finger, the company gave him the job as luggage man on the ship. He had been transferred to the *Princess Victoria* from the *Princess Margaret* while the latter was in dry dock. William was last seen sitting in the ship smoking his pipe, having given his life jacket to a passenger.

### James Mayne (L)

James was an assistant steward on the ship and lived at Curran Street in Larne. His body was washed up on the south coast of the Isle of Man a few days after the loss. During World War Two he served with the Royal Navy and was the holder of the Burma Star. James had previously been a carriage builder and, on being demobbed from the Navy, had joined the *Princess Victoria*. He was single and was a member of the Larne British Legion.

### Gerald Morgan (L)

Gerald was a steward on the ship. He lived at Beechwood Avenue in Stranraer with his wife and young family. Gerald was aged 33 years and had joined the cross-channel route in 1937.

### James A Morrow (L)

James, who was 33 years of age, was an assistant purser on the ship. He came from Carnalbana in Bally-mena. James had attended Larne Grammar School and the Belfast Mercantile College before joining the cross-channel ferries. He was posted to the *Princess Margaret* and was transferred to the *Princess Victoria* in 1949.

### John Murdoch (S)

John, an able seaman on the ship, lived at St Andrew Street in Stranraer He had been at sea for 16 years and had served on the *Princess Victoria* since 1947. John had assisted with the unsuccessful attempt to close the rear stern doors. As the ship was nearing the point of sinking, he helped release two of the lifeboats and escaped the sinking in lifeboat number 6.

### Douglas Murray (L)

Douglas, aged 43 years, was a greaser on the ship and lived at Glynn Road in Larne. He was married with two children and had been a member of the crew for many years. During World War Two he had served on the *Princess Margaret* when the ship was involved in the evacuation at Dunkirk, for which he was awarded the War Medal. Douglas had a passion for motorbikes and it was therefore a sad irony when his body was washed up at Douglas beach on the Isle of Man a few days after the loss. When his body was recovered, it was noticed that the wristwatch he had been wearing was still working. Douglas was the brother-in-law of the purser of the *Princess Victoria*, Hugh Brennan.

### Angus M Nelson (S)

Angus had been at sea for 29 years and had served on the ship since 1947. He was ordered forward by the captain to try to release the bow rudder, but due to the severe weather he was unable to operate it. He escaped the sinking in lifeboat number 6.

### Archibald O'Neill (L)

Archibald was a steward on the ship and came from Glynnview Avenue in Larne. He had worked in the kitchen in the Laharna Hotel in the town. He was single and aged around 27.

### William Parker (L)

William, aged 35, was from Waterloo Road, Larne, and served as a second steward on the ship. He was a native of Castle Kennedy in Scotland and was married with three children, but had lived in Larne for about 12 years. Initially he started on the Princess ships as a pantry boy, when he was aged 15, and had worked his way up to his present position. During his 20 years' service, he had been on the *Princess Maud* at Dunkirk and at the Normandy invasion. William was described as always being well dressed, very popular and very generous and kind.

### John Peoples (L)

John, of Recreation Road in Larne, was the mess room steward on the ship. He was one of a family of six children. Following primary school, John attended Larne Technical College. He was a member of Larne Town Unionist Accordion Band. Jack, as his family called him, pleaded with his parents to be allowed to go to sea like his elder brother, to which they eventually agreed. He was aged 16 years and ten months and was the youngest member of the crew. He had joined the *Princess Victoria* in July 1951. Jack was very keen on cycling and had purchased a new bike just a few weeks before the loss of the ship. He would take the bike with him onto the ship.

### John Porter (L)

John was the third engineer on the ship and lived at Royal Avenue, Stranraer. A married man, he had been a refrigerator engineer and sailed widely. He had joined the cross-channel service in 1948.

### Edward Pritchard (L)

Edward was an assistant cook on the ship and lived at Mountvernon Road in Stranraer. He was recently married. Edward's body was later recovered in one of the ship's lifeboats that was washed ashore at Kearney Point in County Down.

### James S Rankin (L)

James had been at sea on the cross-channel route for the previous 20 years, and was one of the greasers in the engine room. He was married and lived at Murrayfield Gardens, Stranraer.

### Allan Ross (L)

Allan was a second steward on the ship and lived at his parents' hotel in Church Street, Stranraer. He joined the cross-channel route as a galley boy in 1942. He was married with two children. Allan's body was washed up at the south side of the Isle of Man.

### Patrick Shields (L)

Patrick, who was in his late twenties, was an assistant steward on the ship and lived at Roddens Terrace, Larne. He had trained in restaurants in London and Paris before joining the cross-channel service. Patrick had also worked in the kitchen of the Laharna Hotel in Larne, and was described by colleagues as a real character.

### John Taylor (L)

John was the second engineer on the ship. He was originally from Regent Park Grove in Morecambe, England.

### Albert J Thomas (L)

Albert was the ship's chief engineer and came from Fairhurst Avenue, Stranraer. He served on the *Princess Victoria*'s predecessor when she was mined in 1940. He was married with a grown-up son.

### Charles E Thompson (S)

Charles, from St John Street, Stranraer, was a second steward on the ship, aged 23. He had served on the *Princess Victoria* since 1949, and had previously been in the merchant service for five years. Charles was part of a group that were ordered to try and bale out the water that had entered the forward lounge. As the ship was starting to turn over he assisted passengers over the rails. He then slid down the side of the hull and fell into lifeboat number 2 and was rescued by HMS *Contest*.

### John Wallace (L)

John, who was in his twenties, was one of the night stewards on the ship. He lived at Agnew Crescent, Stranraer, but originally came from Kilmarnock. John was married with a son and a daughter. He was a keen fisherman and also kept bees and would provide the honey at local fairs. He joined the route in 1948 as a night steward and was responsible for tending to the passengers who arrived on board the ship during the evening prior to sailing. On the morning of 31 January an additional steward was required and John and a fellow steward, Mr Steele, tossed a coin to see who would sail. John lost the toss and sailed.

### Leonard Arthur White (L)

Leonard, who lived at West Point, Ballygally, was the second officer on the ship. He came originally from London and it was there that his remains were taken for cremation. Leonard was married with three children.

# Passengers on the Princess Victoria

### Robert Baillie (S)

Robert, aged 32, was employed by Short Brothers and Harland as an aircraft riveter at the Wig Bay factory. He lived at Enfield Drive, Belfast. Robert escaped from the ship by jumping into the water and climbing onto a raft. He was rescued by HMS *Contest* and disembarked at Belfast harbour in the evening of 31 January.

### Frederick WB Baird (S)

Billy, as he was known to his family, was aged 38. He lived at Upper Greenisland, County Antrim and was married with two boys. Billy was a company director at the Brookefield Mill in Belfast and was returning from a business trip to Belgium to purchase flax. His ordeal on the ship did not put him off the sea, as he travelled the same route six weeks later. He also had a boat moored on the Shannon. Billy died in 1999.

### Walter Baker (S)

Walter was on national service with the Royal Inniskilling Fusiliers and was travelling to camp. His home address was Milne Road, Rochdale, Lancashire.

### John Vaughan Beer (S)

Chief Petty Officer John Beer, aged 27, was attached to the Fleet Air Arm and was travelling to the Royal Naval base at Eglinton, County Londonderry. He jumped from the ship as it went down and managed to climb onto a raft. After some considerable time on the raft in the open sea, he was rescued by the trawler *Eastcoates* and transferred to the Donaghadee lifeboat which safely landed him at Donaghadee at 01.30 on 1 February. John resided at Strathnairne Street, Cardiff.

### DAN Bilney (L)

Lieutenant Commander Douglas Bilney of the Royal Navy was travelling with his wife to take up a posting at the Royal Naval base at Eglinton, County Londonderry. His body was washed up at Castletown in the Isle of Man several days after the sinking.

### Rebecca Hayes Thompson Bilney (L)

Rebecca, also known as Ruby, was travelling with her husband, Lieutenant Commander AN Bilney. She was the daughter of Mr and Mrs J Milliken who lived in the Dundonald area of Belfast. Her body was recovered at sea and brought to Belfast by the SS *Ballygowan*.

### Geoffrey Bingley (S)

Geoffrey was on national service with the Royal Irish Fusiliers, based at Armagh. He had been granted leave to visit his mother, who lived in London and was unwell, and was now travelling back to his training depot. As the ship was turning over he jumped into lifeboat number 6 which contained the majority of those rescued. He was picked up by the Donaghadee lifeboat. Following the loss, Geoffrey was granted seven days' leave from the Fusiliers.

### Thompson Bonnar (L)

Thompson, who was in his late forties, was a greaser on the sister ship *Princess Margaret* but was here travelling as a passenger. He was married and lived at Mill Street, Larne, where his wife ran a confectionery shop.

### William Ferguson Borland (L)

Bill Borland was a married man who lived at Belmont Road in Stranraer. It was while serving with the RAF in Northern Ireland in World War Two that he had met his wife. They had been married for just 16 months. By trade an upholsterer, Bill was probably best known as the scoutmaster of the 1st Wigtownshire troop. The local newspaper stated that he came to scouting with all the zest of youth, a zest that was never to leave him. The Chief Scout, Lord Rowallan, in a message of sympathy said that scouts would have to accept his loss in the spirit of the Eighth Scout Law, which enjoins them to smile and whistle under all difficulties. Bill had been travelling to Ireland to attend the funeral of his wife's uncle.

### Samuel Harris Brown (L)

Samuel lived on the Antrim Road in Belfast and was married with three daughters. He was well known in the clothing trade and had been returning from a business trip to Great Britain. His body was recovered and landed at Londonderry by the MV *Fredor* a few days after the loss.

### Nancy Adair Bryson (L)

Mrs Nancy Bryson, nee Pollock, who was in her forties, was a native of Londonderry where she had been a co-founder of the Londonderry Christian Workers Union. She and her husband Edgar had been missionaries for 17 years and were on furlough from the African mission field. The family (they had three daughters) were due to return to Kenya in the middle of February 1953. They had been spending time with her sisters at Castlerock and Nancy had gone to Scotland to visit a friend and was returning home on the *Princess Victoria*. Her husband had travelled to Larne to meet her.

### Eileen Carlin (L)

Eileen was travelling with her husband James Carlin.

### James Matthew Carlin (S)

James, who came from St Ninian Place, Prestwick, was travelling with his wife, mother-in-law and sister-in-law on a motoring holiday to Northern Ireland. He was aged 35 and was a civil servant. Due to the heavy winds it proved impossible to load his car at Stranraer. Prior to the ship turning over, he had managed to get his family group onto the deck and up onto the rails, but they were swept away by a large wave. He jumped into lifeboat number 6.

### William Carter (L)

William, who was aged 35 and came from Carncastle, Larne, was a steward on the sister ship, the *Princess Margaret*, but was travelling here as a passenger.

### Joyce Childs (L)

Joyce, who was aged 24, was travelling with her husband Leslie and son Stephen.

### Leslie Childs (L)

Leslie was a chief petty officer in the Royal Navy. His address was Green Road, Southsea, England. Leslie was travelling with his wife and three-year-old son to a new posting on the newly completed Harland and Wolff aircraft carrier HMS *Centaur*, which was due to be handed over to the Navy in September 1953. The Childs family intended to stay with friends at Ranfurley Drive, Belfast. They were interred at Dundonald Cemetery in the suburbs of Belfast.

### Stephen Childs (L)

Three-year-old Stephen was travelling with his father Leslie and mother Joyce.

### Thomas Clark (L)

Thomas, although travelling as a passenger on this occasion, was a mess room steward attached to the *Princess Margaret*. He was aged 19 and lived at Owenstown, Ballysnod, Larne. Thomas had been at sea for only a few years and was travelling home to Larne to arrange insurance for his motorcycle.

## George Herbert Clarke (L)

George, who lived at Cooperative Street, Derby, had travelled to Northern Ireland to visit his mother Winifred, who lived in Hillsborough Parade, Belfast. He was intending to take her back to Derby. George was buried in Dundonald Cemetery.

## James Clements (S)

James lived at Coastguard Cottages, Larne, and was an able seaman on the *Princess Margaret*. He had been at sea for 44 years. During the sinking he was to assist passengers onto the deck and helped to ready a lifeboat for launching. James escaped from the ship in lifeboat number 6 and was picked up by the Donaghadee lifeboat. He continued to work at sea until he died in 1967.

## Harry W Coleman (L)

Harry, who was aged 38, was married and resided at Drains Bay, Larne. He was the company secretary of Henry McNeill Ltd, Main Street, Larne, and was on a business trip to Edinburgh for his firm. Harry had previously worked for the Great Northern Railway (Ireland) and Union Club in Belfast.

## Marie Connery (L)

Marie, who was aged 40 and from Carrick Drive North in Glasgow, was travelling with her mother, sister and brother-in-law James Carlin. When her body was recovered she had in her possession 36 £20 notes.

## Mary Connery (L)

Mary was travelling with her daughters Marie (with whom she lived) and Eileen and her son-in-law James Carlin. In December 1953, James went to court to have Mary legally declared dead, as her body was never recovered.

## Robert McNair Connolly (L)

Robert was an electrician who had been employed for two years by Short Brothers and Harland at their Wig Bay factory.

He was aged 36 and lived at Mary Street, Newtownards, with his wife Eileen and seven-year-old son. He should have journeyed home to Newtownards the previous weekend, but his plans had to be changed at the last minute, resulting in him travelling on the *Princess Victoria*.

## Samuel Cooper (S)

Samuel, from Sallagh Park Central, Larne, was a fireman on the sister ship *Princess Margaret* and was travelling on this crossing as a passenger. As the ship was turning over, Cooper was pushed over the side by William Dummigan, his crew-mate on the *Princess Margaret*. He left the ship in lifeboat number 6.

## William LT Copley (S)

William Copley was a fitter employed at the aircraft factory of Short Brothers and Harland at Wig Bay. He lived at Alliance Avenue in Belfast, and had been married a month earlier. Like his other Shorts' colleagues, he was making his way home on a free travel pass. At one stage, while living in Scotland, William had stood for election as a local councillor. He escaped from the ship by climbing onto one of the rafts and was rescued by the Portpatrick lifeboat. Following the sinking he was off work for six weeks, before returning to the Shorts' factory at Wig Bay.

### Robert Craig (L)

Rab, as he was known, was aged 49. He had run away to sea when he was only 14 years of age. His parents had tried to get him to become a cabinet maker, but nothing would keep him from the sea. He was a fireman on the *Princess Margaret*, but was travelling as a passenger on this occasion. Rab lived at Upper Waterloo Road, Larne. While the *Princess Margaret* was in dry dock in Wales, he had stayed on the ship and had travelled home the previous weekend on a free pass. A fellow crewmate was due to travel on this particular weekend but offered his pass to Rab. He left behind his wife Maggie, three girls and one boy.

### Elizabeth Crawford (L)

Elizabeth was in her late forties and married with three daughters and one son. She lived at Galgorm Street, Ballymena, and was employed as a housekeeper for a family outside the town. Elizabeth had been on a visit to Cairnryan to see her husband who was a captain in the Pioneer Corps there. They had travelled the short distance to Stranraer on the Friday night, where her husband saw her safely onto the ship.

### James Curry (L)

James was married with three children and was an employee of Short Brothers and Harland, working at the Wig Bay factory. He lived at Roden Street in Belfast. James was a cousin of Victor Mitchell who was also lost when the ship sank.

### Thomas Ronald Curry (S)

Thomas, who lived at Donard Drive, Lisburn, was a chargehand electrician at Short Brothers and Harland's Wig Bay factory, where he had worked for the previous two years. He was 34 years of age. During the last two years, Thomas had been a frequent traveller on the *Princess Victoria*. He assisted the crew in handing out life jackets and also helped women up onto the deck. As the ship was sinking he made his way along the upturned keel and jumped into the safety of lifeboat number 6.

### Robert Deans (S)

Robert, who was aged 27, was a labourer from Mains, Stewarton. He was married to a girl from Aghadowey in County Londonderry. He and his friend Albert Dickie were travelling together to have a holiday in Northern Ireland. Robert later emigrated to Australia.

### Albert Dickie (S)

Albert, the youngest child of a family of 16, was aged 26 and was a lance corporal with the Royal Corps of Signals. He lived at Ardreagh Terrace, Aghadowey. Albert was on leave from his regiment in Germany and had travelled often to his home in Scotland with his friend Robert Deans. When he returned to his regiment, following the sinking, he was billed by the army for the uniform and kit he had lost. Albert later said that he spent the rest of his army service in debt paying for the lost equipment. He was married with one daughter.

### Violet Dingle (L)

Miss Violet Dingle was a 19-year-old Wren whose home address was at Enfield in London. She had joined the service six months previously and had just completed her training. She was now travelling to HMS *Sea Eagle* at Londonderry.

### A Doak (S)

Mr A Doak who survived is one of the mystery people who travelled on the ship. From my research, I believe he was the stowaway on board, who was deserting from the army. He had travelled from Euston station on the boat train and survived the sinking. He used this name as an alias.

### Catherine Driver (L)

Catherine, who was aged 32, lived at Earlston Avenue, Glasgow, and was married. She was travelling on the ship with her husband Patrick to visit her sister.

**Patrick Driver (S)**

Patrick also lived in Glasgow. He was married to Catherine Driver, and later had the heart-rending task of identifying her body.

**William Dummigan (L)**

William was a married man from Newington Avenue in Larne. Aged 65, he had been a greaser on the *Princess Margaret* and was travelling home on the *Princess Victoria* to start his retirement.

**Edwin John Fitzgerald (L)**

Edwin was a married man in his early thirties, who lived at Oliver Plunkett Avenue, Dun Laoghaire, Republic of Ireland. He was serving in the British army and was returning home on leave. He was last seen in the third class lounge of the ship.

**John Fitzpatrick (S)**

John, who was aged 25, was a railway fireman employed by British Railways. He lived in Lowther Street, Workington. When the ship sank, John managed to swim to a life raft, was washed off by the heavy waves, but managed to climb back onto it. He was one of the last to be rescued, at around 5.00 pm, by the Donaghadee lifeboat.

**Ernest FW Flack (S)**

Ernest Flack was aged 42 and lived at Laharna Avenue in Larne. He was a production manager employed by the Pye Works in the town. He had been to Cambridge on a business trip and boarded the ship about an hour before it sailed. As the ship sank he climbed onto the side and then the keel of the vessel and jumped into lifeboat number 6. He was then rescued by the Donaghadee lifeboat.

**David RJ Francey (L)**

David, aged 20, came from Moneymore in County Londonderry. He had qualified as a radio operator from the Marine Radio College at Eglantine Avenue in Belfast, and had just been posted to go to sea on the MV *Empire Wansbeck* which was based in Hull. The ship was undergoing sea trials and David had decided to take a short break home.

**Thomas Gault (L)**

Thomas, or Tommy as he was better known, was aged 43 and was the manager of the Leaf Department at Gallaher's cigarette factory in Belfast. He lived at Martinez Avenue in Belfast with his wife. He travelled widely for the firm and had been to England on a business trip. Tommy had been due to fly home but the flight was cancelled due to bad weather. Instead, he travelled on the boat train from London to travel on the *Princess Victoria*. When his body was recovered, a water-stained photograph of his wife was found in his pocket

**David Gillanders (L)**

David, a civil servant, lived in Benton, Northumberland. He was 26 years of age, and was travelling to his family home in Charaville, Enniskillen, to visit his mother.

**James Gilmore (S)**

James, aged 32, was an administration manager at the Wig Bay factory of Short Brothers and Harland. He was making his monthly trip to see his wife at the family home at Crumlin Road in Belfast. He was rescued from a raft by Petty Officer Wilfred Warren from HMS *Contest* who dived into the water to bring him to the safety of the destroyer. He was immediately taken to the boiler room on the destroyer to warm up after his time in the water. In August 1941 Gilmore had been presented with a Royal Humane Society award for carrying out a rescue in Donaghadee harbour when he saved a young boy who had fallen into the water.

### Mary Gunn (L)

Molly, as she was known, was originally from Newcastle-upon-Tyne and had come to live in Draperstown following her marriage in August 1952. She and her husband both taught in the local school and Molly was only a few months pregnant. She was returning to Draperstown after attending the funeral of an uncle in her home town in England

### David W Hamilton (L)

David, aged 22 years, worked in Newmills in Ayrshire and was making a surprise visit to his parents who lived at Gortin near Carnlough in County Antrim. He was also going to say a farewell to his brother who was emigrating to Canada. David's body was recovered in the North Channel five weeks after the loss of the ship by the SS *Ballyalton*, a collier en route from Whitehaven to Portaferry. Papers found in his clothing bore the name DW Hamilton. His remains were taken ashore at Donaghadee.

### William Allen Hammond (L)

William, who was aged 23, was an electrical inspector at the Wig Bay aircraft factory of Short Brothers and Harland. He lived at Little Victoria Street in Belfast. William had been a member of the 15th Belfast Scouts and was described as being a lively character.

### Jane Hanna (L)

Jane was a widow who lived at Troopers Lane in Carrickfergus. She had one daughter and two granddaughters. Jane had been to Glasgow to visit an aunt and sent her daughter a letter telling her that she would be home on Saturday and to meet her at the railway station at Carrickfergus. In her letter she said that she would have some presents for her granddaughters. The family waited at the station and were later told about the loss of the ship. Jane was a prominent member of the Carrickfergus Women's Unionist Association.

### Robert Harpur (S)

Robert, aged 32 years, came originally from Glasgow and was well known in Belfast as he played for Linfield Football Club (he had also played football for Partick Thistle, Ayr United, Queen of the South and Southend). On this occasion he was travelling to play with Linfield in a friendly match against Airdrie. The match was cancelled as the Scottish team could not leave Renfrew Airport due to winds in excess of 85 mph. Robert said that it was a pathetic sight to see men, women and children clinging with their frozen fingers to the port side rails of the ship. When the order came to abandon the ship, they started to slide down the side of the ship into the water. He was one of the last to leave the ship and slid into a lifeboat. He was washed out of that boat but was pulled into boat number 6 by John McKnight, chief cook of the *Princess Victoria*. Robert died in 1980.

### Kenneth B Harrison (S)

Kenneth, from Settle in Skipton, was aged 19 and was on national service. As the ship was sinking he climbed over the side, jumped into the sea and was pulled into lifeboat number 6.

### Joseph Hastings (S)

Joseph was a fitter at the Wig Bay aircraft factory belonging to Short Brothers and Harland. He was aged 37 and lived at Bann Street in Belfast. He was married with

a family of three boys and two girls. Joseph had served with the RAF in North Africa during World War Two and afterwards had worked at Shorts as a fitter. He was not scheduled to make a trip home on this particular weekend, but his son was ill in hospital and he was given permission to visit him. After the loss of the ship he continued working at Shorts until he retired in 1973. Joseph died in April 1998.

### Adam Heggarty (L)

Adam, who was aged 23, lived at Gloucester Avenue in Larne and was a steward on the *Princess Margaret*. He was engaged to Phillomena McDowall who was also travelling to Larne to see Adam's family. Phillomena was also lost. They had planned to marry in March 1953.

### Annie VE Jackson MBE (L)

Miss Annie Jackson lived at Eglantine Avenue in Belfast. She was a senior inspector of domestic science for the Ministry of Education in Northern Ireland and was returning home following a conference of domestic science officials in Edinburgh. Annie had been awarded the MBE in 1945. Her body was washed ashore a week after the loss at Whithorn Bay, Wigtownshire. At her funeral the Reverend Withers stated that "she was a woman of character and courage whose personality bound people to her in unending friendship".

### Frank Jewhurst (L)

Frank, who was a captain and adjutant of the 53rd AA Workshop Company, REME, lived at Cherryhill Drive in Dundonald outside Belfast. He was aged 60 and married. The family had previously lived in Holywood where his son played for a local football team.

### Florence Johnstone (L)

Florence lived at Rushfield Avenue in Belfast. She had been on a visit to see her husband Robert who worked at the Short Brothers and Harland Wig Bay factory. She had travelled back on the ship herself. Her husband flew back to Northern Ireland on the following day to try to discover any news of her fate.

### Robert Kelly (L)

Robert was a fitter who lived at Wallasey Park in Belfast. He was married.

### James Kerr (S)

James was a captain on one of Kelly's coal boats, the *Ballygilbert*. He lived on the Serpentine Road in Belfast. James stated later that he knew that something was gravely wrong with the ship. He assisted with releasing lifeboat number 6 and as the ship sank he got into it. As an experienced seafarer, James ensured that the lifeboat's sea anchor was deployed.

### Dudley Farnsworth Kipling (L)

Dudley, who was in his sixties, was a director of Welch, Margetson and Company, shirt manu-facturers of Londonderry, where he also lived. He was returning from a business trip to London. Dudley was married with a daughter and two sons, one of whom had been killed in World War Two. He had joined the company in 1906 and was transferred to Londonderry in 1939. During the war he had been attached to the local Home Guard as an intelligence officer. Dudley was a distant relative of Rudyard Kipling and a member of the Londonderry Rotary Club.

### James Edwin Lowe BEM (L)

James was a flight sergeant in the Royal Air Force. He was married with a young daughter and lived at Flush Green in Belfast. James was aged 50 and had served in the forces since he was 16. He was travelling home from Bedford. His wife later brought the first claim for damages to the Northern Ireland High Court following the loss.

### Thomas J Lowther (L)

Thomas was a flight inspector with Short Brothers and Harland at the Wig Bay factory. Like 22 other passengers, he was travelling home on a free weekend pass. Thomas lived at Loopland Park in Belfast with his wife and twin daughters.

### Donal McAteer (S)

Donal was an electrician employed by the Swan Hunter shipyard at Newcastle-upon-Tyne, normally travelling home to Thorburn Road, Belfast, every two months. He was involved in rescuing some passengers who had become trapped in the dining room as the ship was in the final throws of sinking. He was rescued from a lifeboat by HMS *Contest*.

### Dominic Francis McCarter (L)

Dominic was a passenger who came from Walmer Street in Belfast. He was married.

### Mr McClatchey (L)

Mr McClatchey was from Belfast and was an employee of Short Brothers and Harland's Wig Bay factory

### Robert McClean (S)

Robert was married with five children and came from Ballyness East, Bushmills. He had been working in England but had left his job and was returning home to find employment in Northern Ireland.

### William McClenaghan (L)

Billy, as he was known, was aged 28 and lived at Carryduff, just outside Belfast. He had been married for only ten months and his wife was expecting their first child. He was employed as a chargehand electrician by Short Brothers and Harland at the Wig Bay factory where he had spent most of his working life. Billy was interested in sport, playing cricket for Saintfield Cricket Club and also playing golf regularly. As the ship sank, he jumped into the water and swam about. One of the lifeboats tried to reach him but was unsuccessful.

### Alexander McCready (L)

Sandy, as he was known, was aged 61 years and lived at Ballylumford, Islandmagee. He was a quartermaster on the *Princess Margaret* and was travelling home as a passenger on weekend leave. During World War Two he had been quartermaster on the *City of Manchester*, which was torpedoed off Java. He was then held as a prisoner of war for three and a half years. Sandy was married with two sons.

### Alfred McCready (L)

Alfred lived at Greyabbey Road, Ballywalter, with his wife and three children. He had left his family home only nine weeks previously to find work in Scotland.

### Ian McDonald (L)

Ian, aged 28, was a clerk at Stranraer railway station and lived at Broomfield Gardens in the town. He was travelling to his family home in Ballyhalbert, County Down. Ian was married with a young son.

### Phillomena McDowall (L)

Phillomena was aged 19 and engaged to steward Adam Heggarty. They were both travelling on the ship. She lived at Whitsun Avenue, Stranraer.

### David Peter Megarry (S)

David, who was in his mid-twenties, was an electrician employed at the Shorts' aircraft factory at Wig Bay. This was his third crossing on the ship. He lived at Millfort Avenue in Dunmurry. As the ship was sinking he jumped into the water and swam to a lifeboat. He clung to one of the lines hanging from the boat and after some minutes managed to get his leg over the side and was hauled in. Another man was also hanging on a rope beside Megarry, but he slipped off and was drowned.

### James Alexander McKay (L)

James was an electrical inspector employed at the Shorts' aircraft factory at Wig Bay. He lived at North Approach Road in Belfast and was married.

### Patrick Joseph McLaughlin (L)

Patrick, who was more commonly known as Joe, was aged 29 years and lived at Dungloe, County Donegal, with his wife and three children. By trade he was a butcher. Joe had gone to England to try and find employment, but had been unsuccessful. He then decided to return to Ireland and wrote to his wife telling her of his plans. The letter was posted before he made the journey to Stranraer and was delivered a few days after the loss of the ship.

### R McLaughlin (L)

Mr McLaughlin was a passenger who lived at Cullingtree Road in Belfast.

### Andrew McMurtry (L)

Andrew, who was aged 56, was the ship's carpenter on the *Princess Margaret* and was travelling home for weekend leave. He lived at Drummond Street, Larne, and was married with one son. He had assisted the ship's crew in their failed attempt to close the breached stern doors. Following his efforts he had collapsed on the car deck and had to be assisted back to the lounge. He had fought in World War One and had been at sea for most of his life.

### Agnes Mary McNeill (L)

Nan, as she was known to her family, was pregnant and was travelling with her husband Ronald.

### Ronald George McNeill (L)

Ronald was a fitter employed at the Shorts' aircraft factory at Wig Bay. He was travelling to his family home at Ava Drive, Belfast, along with his wife. When the ship sank he had got into one of the lifeboats. He saw his wife in the water and dived in to save her. Even though he was a strong swimmer, and reached his wife, the waves overcame them, and both were lost.

### Samuel McMaster McReynolds (L)

Samuel, aged 37, was an electrician employed at the Short Brothers and Harland aircraft factory at Wig Bay, and had worked there for nearly two years. He lived at Rosebrook, Carrickfergus, with his wife and eight children.

### Margaret Magee (L)

Margaret, who was aged 20, was originally from Drumraymond, Toomebridge. She had worked in London for the previous 12 months and her plans had been to travel home on the Heysham to Belfast ferry, but she missed the boat train in London for the Heysham boat and instead decided to travel on the *Princess Victoria*. She had sent a telegram to her brother-in-law Robert McLean, who worked in the Grand Central Hotel in Belfast, informing him of her change of travel plans. She had previously been employed in a cafe in Ballymena and was one of eight children.

### Helen Magill (L)

Helen, a native of Blackley, Manchester, was aged 35 years and was travelling with her husband John.

### John Arthur Magill (L)

John, who had addresses in both Portpatrick and Whitewell Drive, Belfast, was travelling with his wife Helen. The couple had only been married about three months. John was a senior inspector with Short Brothers and Harland at the Wig Bay factory and was well known in motorcycling circles in Northern Ireland. His body was later recovered by the coastal vessel *Snow Queen*.

### Richard Mason (L)

Richard was a works foreman who worked and lived temporarily in London. He was travelling home to see his wife at the family home at Markethill, County Armagh.

### Isabella Sarah Milligan (L)

Isabella was in her sixties and had one daughter. She lived at Tobermore Road, Magherafelt, and was returning home from a trip to England. This was only the second occasion she had been on a ship.

### Victor Mitchell (L)

Victor, who was aged 30, was an electrician employed by Short Brothers and Harland at the Wig Bay factory. He lived at Espie Way in Belfast and was married with young children. Victor was a cousin of James Curry, a fellow passenger who was also lost when the ship sank.

### Iris M Mooney (L)

Iris was returning to her home at Knocktayde View in Ballycastle with her two children, John and Kevin. She had been on a holiday to visit her mother who lived in Newcastle-upon-Tyne. Iris was married and her husband was a lorry driver who was 43 years of age. She had originally planned to travel the previous weekend, but had been forced to change her travel plans as one of her sons was unwell. Following the loss of the ship, her husband John lodged a claim for the loss of his wife and children. He was awarded £1,350 by the court: £750 for the loss of his wife and £600 for the loss of his two children.

### John Noble Mooney (L)

John, who was aged five years, was travelling with his mother and younger brother.

### Kevin Mooney (L)

Kevin, who was aged two years, was travelling with his mother and elder brother.

### Hubert J Moore (L)

Hubert, who was in his late forties, was an employee of Short Brothers and Harland at the Wig Bay factory. He was travelling home to Richardson Street in Belfast with his wife and young son.

### Martha Moore (L)

Mrs Moore was travelling with her husband and son. She had previously been a widow with a young family and had remarried. She had worked for Shorts Brothers and Harland and it was there that she met her second husband.

### Victor Moore (L)

Victor, who was aged eight years, was travelling with his parents.

**James Morrow (L)**

James lived at Roddens Lane in Larne.

**Thomas Morton (L)**

Thomas was an employee of the Short Brothers and Harland factory at Wig Bay and was travelling home on his free pass to Ainsworth Avenue in Belfast. He was married with one daughter.

**Francis Mullan (L)**

Frank, who was aged 29, was a sergeant in the Royal Inniskilling Fusiliers, in which he had served for seven and a half years. His mother, who lived at Ballymully, Limavady, had been unwell for some time and Frank was given compassionate leave to travel home from his posting in East Africa. He was to be transferred to Omagh Barracks. His family were unaware that he was on the ship until they were informed by the Royal Ulster Constabulary. His body was found in a lifeboat belonging to the *Princess Victoria* that was washed up at Kearney Point near Portaferry three days after the sinking of the ship.

**Rose Mary Mullan (L)**

Rose Mary, who was one of 11 children, was a student nurse at Warlingham Park Hospital in Surrey. She was aged 22 years and was travelling home to see her parents who lived at Garvagh, County Londonderry. She had taken up nursing in May 1951 and had been unable to travel home at Christmas due to having to sit examinations.

**John Gerald Murray (S)**

John was an electrical fitter employed at the aircraft factory at Wig Bay. He lived at Devonshire Street in Belfast. As the ship was sinking, he escaped by jumping into the sea and climbing onto a raft and was later picked up by HMS *Contest*.

**Joseph O'Connor (L)**

Joseph, who was aged 65, was a doctor who lived in Gateshead, Northumberland. He was a native of Carrickmacross in the Republic of Ireland. His body was taken south from the Belfast City Morgue, with more than 100 cars joining the cortege at Dundalk.

**William Nassau Parker (L)**

Willie, as he was known to his family, was a fitter employed at the Wig Bay aircraft factory. He lived at Ava Gardens, Belfast, and was married.

**Wolsey William Patterson (L)**

Wolsey was married in 1952 to a girl from Edinburgh and they lived at West Street, Carrickfergus. He had served in the RAF as a radio operator and after being demobbed was employed by Short Brothers and Harland at the Belfast factory. Several months previously he had been transferred to the Wig Bay factory. Wolsey had intended to bring his wife Davina on the voyage, but changed his mind at the last minute.

**Denis Peck (S)**

Denis, from Saxmunden, Suffolk, was on national service attached to the North Irish Horse regiment, based at Belfast. He was returning to duty. This was the first time he had crossed on this route. Denis was rescued from lifeboat number 6 by the Donaghadee lifeboat.

### Alex Petrie (L)

Alex, who was aged 28, was a flight sergeant in the RAF and came from Loch Ryan Street, Stranraer. He had previously been a policeman in the Dumfries and Galloway Constabulary.

### John Spence Piggot (L)

Spence, who was aged 28 years, had just recently been made a director in the Inglis Bakery in Belfast and was returning from a business trip with his brother to London. He lived with his brother Lennox at the family home. As the ship was starting to turn over on its side, Lennox was terribly seasick in his cabin. Spence went up to the deck to find out what was happening and told Lennox that he would come back for him. Spence was lost as the ship turned over and was unable to return for his brother.

### Lennox Donald Piggot (L)

Lennox, aged 19 years, lived at Osbourne Gardens, Belfast, and worked at the Inglis Bakery in the city. His father was chairman of the company. Lennox had been at an exhibition in London with his brother Spence and both were returning home. They were scheduled to fly back to Belfast, but due to the bad weather the flight was cancelled and they decided to travel home on the *Princess Victoria*.

### Eileen Sylvia Prentice (L)

Miss Prentice came from Downe, Farnborough. She was a Wren who had just completed her training and was travelling to her first posting at HMS *Sea Eagle* in Londonderry. She had left Reading train station the previous evening to make the journey to Stranraer.

### Ada E Prior (L)

Ada came from The Bay in Carnlough. She had travelled to London to attend the funeral of her mother. Ada was joint proprietor, with a Miss Lamount, of Green's Cafe in Carnlough. Her body was never recovered and an application was made to the court to have her presumed dead. The application was subsequently granted.

### Adam McCann Reid (L)

Adam lived at Armitage Street, Belfast. He was a labourer employed at the Short Brothers and Harland factory at Wig Bay. Adam was married with a teenage daughter. His body was recovered by the MV *Fredor* a few days after the loss and taken ashore at Londonderry.

### Robert JH Ritchie (L)

Robert, who lived at Newington Avenue, Larne, was aged 22 and was by profession a butcher, having served his apprenticeship at Tom Graham's butchers in Larne. He had been working in England and was returning to Larne. His body was recovered by the SS *Clonlee* off Douglas Head, Isle of Man, five days after the loss. Robert was a member of the Orange Order and was a very keen Lambeg drummer, as well as being interested in pigeon racing.

### Ivan Campbell Robinson (L)

Ivan, aged 37 years, lived at Neely Street, Belfast. He was married with one girl and two boys. He had previously worked for Ewart's Mill in Belfast and then went to work on the railways in England. He was returning to Belfast to arrange for his wife and children to move to England.

### Robert J Rosborough (L)

Robert, who was aged 36, lived at Ogilvie Street in Belfast and had been married in July 1952. He had been to England on a business trip and was returning home.

### John G Ross (S)

John, aged 23 years, lived at Loughmorne, Carrickfergus. He was unemployed and had been to England to try and join the RAF, but had been told that his application was unsuccessful. As the ship was listing badly he assisted some women up the lifelines that had been laid out in the ship. He eventually had to break a window and climb through it to make his escape from the ship. He survived in lifeboat number 6.

### Kenneth T Rotherham (S)

Kenneth was serving in the RAF at the Bishops-court base in County Down. He was aged 22 years and came from Bishop Street, Liverpool. Kenneth escaped the ship in lifeboat number 2 and was rescued by HMS *Contest*.

### AP Rowlands (L)

Mr Rowlands, who was aged 21 years, came from Durranhill, Carlisle. He was a craftsman attached to the REME at Palace Barracks, Holywood, County Down. He was home on leave and was returning to his regiment prior to a posting to the Middle East. Rowlands had married Maureen Henderson of Carlisle two days before travelling on the *Princess Victoria*. He was a former football player with Carlisle United and had played a few matches with the Belfast team Distillery. He also played inside-forward for Trinity Old Boys in the Bangor Summer Football League

### Lily Russell (L)

Lily lived at Kiltoy, Letterkenny, Republic of Ireland. She was unmarried, aged 27 years, and worked in a factory in Carlisle. When the ship sank, Lily managed to jump into the water and then clamber onto a raft along with John Fitzpatrick. She told him her name and that she was travelling to Donegal to visit her sick mother. A heavy wave hit the raft and both of them were washed off into the sea. Fitzpatrick saw Lily clinging to another raft which was then hit by a further wave and she was washed away.

### Gerald J Shankland (L)

Gerald was a chief petty officer in the Royal Navy and came from Hilltop Avenue, Cheshire. His body was later washed up at the Isle of Man.

### J Maynard Sinclair MP (L)

Major Sinclair, who was aged 57, lived at Deramore Park South in Belfast with his wife. He was the Deputy Prime Minister and Minister of Finance in the Northern Ireland government, representing the Cromac ward. His list of credentials was impressive: served in the Royal Irish Rifles from 1916 to 1919; former chairman of the Belfast Savings Bank; a member of the Belfast Harbour Commissioners; and vice president of Linfield Football Club. When the ship was sinking, he assisted some of the children and women up to the boat deck. His mother-in-law, Mrs A Claridge, died on being told the news of his loss. A sports pavilion at Stormont was later named after him.

### Walter D Smiles MP (L)

Lieutenant Colonel Sir Walter Smiles represented the North Down constituency in the Westminster Parliament. He was aged 70 years and was married with one daughter. He lived at Portavoe Point, near Orlock Head in County Down. His aunt was Mrs Beaton who wrote the famous cookery book. Throughout his life he had been active in public life and was the first managing director of the

Belfast Ropeworks. During World War One he was decorated twice with the Distinguished Service Order and was at one stage recommended for a Victoria Cross. When the ship was sinking he was assisted up one of the lifelines that had been laid out in the ship, but he was terribly seasick and told a survivor that he was very weak. He was last seen clinging onto the deck of the ship. From where the ship sank, off the Copeland Islands, in good weather he would have had sight of his own home on the shore. His body was recovered from the Irish Sea by HMS *Contest* on 1 February.

### John R Stanford (S)

John was aged 20 years and came from Midland Road, Kettering. He was a leading stoker in the Royal Navy, attached to HMS *Crispin*. During the sinking he rescued some passengers from the lounge by smashing a window and hauling them up with a rope. As the ship went down he jumped off the keel and landed on a raft and then got into lifeboat number 6.

### George W Sterling (S)

George, who was in his mid-twenties, was an aircraft sprayer employed at the Wig Bay factory. He lived at Cavour Street, Belfast. As the ship turned over he was holding onto the port-side rail. He heard a whistle sound and climbed over the rail, walked along the keel and jumped into lifeboat number 2.

### James Sumner (L)

James was a sergeant in the Royal Inniskilling Fusiliers. He came from Tipperary in the Republic of Ireland. He was returning from a training course in England, which should have finished the previous week but overran. His wife had died in 1952, leaving him with the care of three young children. James was buried in Omagh with full military honours.

### Mr Sweeny (L)

Mr Sweeny was a passenger from the the Dublin area in the Republic of Ireland.

### Albert Tatchel (L)

Albert, who was aged around 50, was a flight sergeant in the RAF and came from Corfelcastle in Devon. He had been married and had two daughters. Albert had recently been demobbed from the RAF and was travelling to Northern Ireland to try to find employment.

### Ivor J Thomas (S)

Ivor, who came from Wygan Place in Cardiff, was aged 22. He had just been posted on national service the previous day to HMS *Gannet* which was based at Eglinton, County Londonderry. As the ship was sinking, he assisted John Stanford in breaking windows in the side of the vessel and rescuing fellow-passengers. He dived into the water as the ship was going down and managed to come up beside lifeboat number 6 and was hauled in.

### James Wallace (S)

James, who was aged 23 years, originally came from Upper Woodburn in Carrickfergus, but was working as a steeplejack in London. He travelled home every month to see his parents, normally via Heysham, but decided this particular weekend to travel from Stranraer. The fare from London was £6 12s (£6.60). When the ship was hit by the first large wave he was standing at the stern and saw the water enter the car deck and also the attempt to close the doors. As the ship was sinking he jumped into lifeboat number 6.

### Robert White (L)

Robert, aged 33, was a manufacturing agent with premises at High Street in Belfast. He lived at Sterling Avenue, Belfast, with his wife and nine-year-old son.

### Norman Willis (L)

Norman was a labourer who came from Severn Street, Belfast. His body was recovered by the MV *Fredor* and landed at Londonderry a few days after the loss.

### George A Wilson (S)

George was aged 25 years and came from Hawkins Street, Londonderry. He was in the Royal Corps of Signals. George was able to climb over the side of the ship and get into lifeboat number 6. He later went on to manage a plastics firm in Gloucester.

### John Alexander Wilton (L)

John was a leading telegraphist on HMS *Sea Eagle* in Londonderry. He was 23 years of age and came from Enfield Street, Portstewart. John had been educated at Coleraine Technical College and had played football for the school team, as well as being a member of Portrush

Sea Cadets. He had travelled to a naval hospital in England for treatment and was returning to his posting. His parents did not know that their son was on the *Princess Victoria*.

### Geraldine Wordsworth (L)

Geraldine was a widow whose husband had been an officer in the army. She had one son and they lived at Menton, Newcastle-upon-Tyne. Geraldine was travelling alone with the intention of visiting her parents who lived in Maghera, County Londonderry. Normally she travelled with her 12-year-old son, but on this occasion she had left the boy at school in England and was travelling alone.

### John S Yeomans (S)

John was on national service and was posted to HMS *Sea Eagle* in Londonderry. He was aged 22 and came from Farnborough. When the ship sank he jumped into the water and swam to a raft, which had a few people on it. John found it difficult to get a place on the raft and swam to another one and was eventually picked up by the Portpatrick lifeboat. He died in 1974.

### Photographic Acknowledgements

The author gratefully acknowledges the kind assistance of the following individuals and organisations in supplying the photographs used in this chapter: L Baird collection; J Baxter collection; *Belfast Telegraph*; L Brady collection; M Brodie collection; Bryson family collection; Cooper family collection; W Copley collection; *County Down Spectator*; B Crawford collection; D Irwin collection; *Larne Times*; P Leahey collection; D Lockhart collection; N McClean collection; McGarry family collection; E Mullan collection; *Newtownards Chronicle*; H Noble collection; *Northern Whig*; M Price collection; PRONI; J Ritchie collection; J Simpson collection; W Smith collection; J Spratt collection; M Thompson collection; J Waring collection; *Wigtown Free Press*; Wordsworth family collection.

# Fated not to sail

Following major disasters like the loss of the *Princess Victoria*, there are always many people who claim to have been booked to travel on the vessel that sank, but cancelled their plans prior to sailing. I was well aware of this syndrome from research on my previous book, *Titanic Belfast's Own*. In that instance there were nearly enough people claiming that they should have been sailing on the *Titanic* to half fill the passenger manifest.

In this research I have discovered one family and five individuals who were due to sail on the *Princess Victoria* on that Saturday morning 50 years ago, but for various reasons had had to cancel their travel arrangements and consequently lived to tell the tell. I feel that while they did not travel on the ship, their tales should be recorded.

### Captain William Kerr

Captain Kerr, who lived in Drains Bay in Larne, was the master of the cargo ship SS *Clonlee* and had left the ship on a week's leave to travel home on the *Princess Victoria*. Business arrangements delayed him in England and instead he travelled home on the Saturday Liverpool to Belfast ferry, arriving in Drains Bay at around midnight.

### The Large Family

Mr and Mrs Victor Large were in the process of moving home from Stranraer to Belfast. They had a family of three girls and two boys and were due to travel on the *Princess Victoria*. On Friday, 30 January their three-year-old son Victor took unwell. The local doctor was called and diagnosed an attack of appendicitis – his advice to Mr Large was not to travel the following day. On the Saturday, Victor was admitted to hospital and the family was left to count their blessings that they took the doctor's advice.

### Attracta McDermott

Attracta lived at Margaret Street in the Waterside, Londonderry. She had travelled to London via the Larne–Stranraer route the previous week to attend the wedding of her brother. She was due to travel back home on the *Princess Victoria* but some relatives persuaded her to stay a few extra days in London. Her parents, unaware of the change in her travel plans, were sure that she had died on the ship. They had an anxious wait until Attracta phoned a relative in Londonderry to let them know she was safe.

### Archie O'Neill

Mr O'Neill, who lived in Bryan Street in Larne, was a member of the crew of the *Princess Victoria* and was due to travel off duty to Larne, but decided instead to stay in Stranraer.

### Robert McClenaghan

Mr McClenaghan, who lived at Ballysnod Road in Larne, was a steward on the *Princess Margaret*. He had travelled with this ship to Holyhead where the vessel was put in dry dock for repairs. When he arrived at Stranraer he decided to spend the weekend in the Scottish port.

### John McFetridge

Mr McFetridge, a holder of the George Medal for service in the war, lived at Point Street in Larne. He was a steward on the *Princess Victoria* and was due to sail with the ship on Friday, 30 January. However, due to his brother-in-law having undergone a serious operation in hospital, John decided to stay and be with his family at that time.

# Remembrance

Messages of sympathy flooded into Northern Ireland and Scotland following the loss of the ship. Her Majesty Queen Elizabeth II led the nation when she sent a message of sympathy to the Minister of Transport, Mr Lennox-Boyd: "I and my husband were greatly distressed to hear of the sinking of the *Princess Victoria*. Will you please convey our deepest sympathy to the relatives of all those who lost their lives in this terrible disaster."

Winston Churchill, the Prime Minister, sent a telegram to Mr John Elliott, the chairman of British Railways: "Please accept sincerest sympathy of my Government, colleagues and myself. We mourn with the bereaved and feel deeply for all involved in this great tragedy." The Prime Minister of Northern Ireland, Lord Brookeborough, issued a statement on behalf of the government in Belfast:

> I am most deeply distressed by the tragic fate of the Princess Victoria involving a grievous toll of life and a terrible ordeal for those who have survived the fury of tempest and sea . . . In the name of the Government of Northern Ireland and on behalf of my wife and myself, I offer sincerest sympathy to the bereaved and to all who in any way have suffered by this heart-rending tragedy.

He later paid a glowing tribute to the people of Donaghadee in a letter to the local council:

> In my broadcast on Sunday evening about the terrible disaster which overtook those who were in the *Princess Victoria* during her last voyage. I had the opportunity of paying tribute to the people of Donaghadee.
>
> I feel I must follow that by a direct expression of my own and my Government's admiration of the splendid work of your townsfolk.
>
> I am sure the generous assistance, comfort and the care bestowed on the survivors of that awful tragedy and the many offers to help will be long remembered and appreciated by them with deepest gratitude.
>
> May I congratulate Donaghadee warmly on the

wholehearted demonstration it gave of true Ulster hospitality and helpfulness.

Messages of condolence were received from Mr RG Menzies, the Prime Minister of Australia; Mr SG Holland, the Prime Minister of New Zealand; Mr Louis St Laurent, the Prime Minister of Canada; and Mr Ralph Boernstein, the Belfast Consul General for the United States. All sent word to Northern Ireland of how much the tragedy had touched them and their fellow countrymen and women. Messages of sympathy were also received from Sir Rupert de la Bere, the Lord Mayor of London, and from Mr Eamon de Valera, President of the Republic of Ireland.

The two towns that were linked by the *Princess Victoria* – Larne and Stranraer – were also to be the two places that suffered the greatest loss of life. The majority of the crew came from the two towns and most of their families knew each other.

On Sunday, 1 February, the day after the tragedy, there was still torrential rain falling in the bitter cold at Donaghadee, but this did not stop hundreds of people gathering in the afternoon at the pier, near the berth of the lifeboat *Sir Samuel Kelly*, to take part in a service to remember those who had been lost only a few hours earlier. The Reverend Thomas Martin, rector of Donaghadee, officiated at the service which was held adjacent to the lighthouse at the end of the pier. Among those represented were members of the Donaghadee lifeboat crew, the Salvation Army and British Railways. Sir Clarence Graham represented the Prime Minister.

Donaghadee Flute Band accompanied those present when they sank the hymn 'Oh God, our Help in Ages Past'. In his address, Reverend Martin said that they had gathered at the pier to seek the Divine presence for all those who were in any way affected by the disaster. They wished, he said, to remember before God all those who had been bereaved in the shipping disaster off their shores and also those who had lost loved ones in England, Holland and elsewhere. Of the people of Donaghadee he said, "Never in all their history had the Donaghadee people displayed such good fellowship and self-sacrifice as they had during the storm." In concluding his address, he spoke directly to those who mourned the loss of a loved one by quoting from St John chapter 14, verse 27: "Peace I leave with you, my peace I give onto you: not as the world giveth, give I unto you. Let not your heart be troubled, neither let it be afraid." For those gathered, Reverend Martin said he prayed "that they would leave the service with gratitude to God and go away with peace, comfort and hope in their hearts".

After the service a minute's silence was held and Captain Thomas Clokey cast the first of many wreaths into the sea. It was from those who had survived the ordeal and bore the inscription: "In loving memory of all those who were lost on the M.V. *Princess Victoria* – from the survivors." The wreath was in the shape of a lifeboat.

On Sunday, 8 February, a week later, many more hundreds of people gathered close to the *Princess Victoria*'s berth in the town of Larne to take part in an act of remembrance. The service was held at the harbour station which would normally have been bustling with activity but was now unnaturally calm as the townspeople gathered. Close by them was the berth where only a week previously had stood the *Princess Victoria*, a berth now empty and silent. Tied up at the wharf was the *Pass of Drumochter*, the oil tanker that had gone to assist in the rescue. Her crew stood on the deck during the service. Like the service at Donaghadee, all of the town's clergy were present and took part in the service. Two brothers of Captain Ferguson were present, as well as many representatives from British Railways. Mr J McKeown, the Permanent Secretary to the Ministry of Commerce, represented the Northern Ireland government, while Larne Council was represented by the Mayor, Alderman Ross MBE.

The service commenced with an opening prayer by the Reverend John Bertenshaw of Larne Methodist Church, followed by the singing of the 23rd Psalm. The lesson was read by the Reverend EA Jones of Larne and Inver. Following this, the hymn 'Abide with Me' was sung, during which the Mayor of Larne, accompanied by representatives, including the Stranraer Council Treasurer Mr JE Budge and William Nelson of the Donaghadee lifeboat, laid the first wreath. As they did so the Mayor said:

We the people of Larne and of Stranraer do cast into the waters these garlands in memory of the master of the vessel *Princess Victoria* and of those of her crew and passengers who perished in the storm of January 31.

The Reverend RVA Lynas of Gardenmore Presbyterian led those gathered in prayer and the Reverend WJ McGeagh of First Larne Presbyterian then gave a short address. He concluded by quoting some lines of poetry:

Spin cheerfully, not tearfully
Though wearily you plod
Spin carefully, spin prayerfully
But leave the thread with God.

The shuttles of His purpose move
To carry out His own design
Seek not too soon to disapprove His work
Nor yet assign dark motives when with
Silent tread you view each sombre fold
For lo, within each darker thread
There twines a thread of gold.

Spin cheerfully, not tearfully,
He knows the way you plod
Spin carefully, spin prayerfully
But leave the thread with God.

Several other wreaths were cast into the water and the service closed with those gathered singing the hymn 'Eternal Father'. This service was broadcast live by BBC Radio in Northern Ireland.

A memorial service was also held in St Anne's Cathedral in Belfast. The Governor of Northern Ireland, Lord Wakehurst, attended, while the Minister of Transport, Mr AT Lennox-Boyd, represented the British government. The service was conducted by the Dean of St Anne's, the Very Reverend RCA Elliott. In his address, which was drawn from the Song of Solomon, the Reverend Cannon RA Deane said, "Many waters cannot quench love, neither can the floods drown it." Referring to the loss of all the women and children, he continued:

It is a noble part of our sea tradition that in the hour of peril the women and children shall be rescued first. It is the most bitter part of our sorrow that this tradition failed, not because anyone sinned against it, but because circumstances compelled its failure.

He concluded his address by remarking:

We would be glad today if by any word or act we could enter into fellowship with the homes that have suffered, for it must be in the great heart of the home the greatest grief is known.

In Belfast's Grosvenor Hall, the Reverend John Montgomery, President of the Methodist Church in Ireland, conducted a service of remembrance. The Minister of Education, Mr H Midgley, represented the Northern Ireland government, while Sir William Neill represented Belfast Corporation. The Reverend Montgomery asked those gathered to respond generously to the recently established Princess Victoria Appeal Fund. On behalf of the Methodist Church he offered their sympathy to all those bereaved.

Later that evening a memorial service was held at Stranraer. The evening service from the Old Parish Church in the town was broadcast by the BBC. The service opened with the singing of the 23rd Psalm. Other hymns sung during the service included 'Jesus, Lover of my Soul' and 'O Love that will not let me go'. At the conclusion of the service the choir sank the anthem 'Cast thy burden on the Lord' and the address was given by the Reverend Russell Walker.

Two days after the loss, the *Princess Maud*, sister ship to the *Princess Victoria*, slowly made her way up Loch Ryan towards her berth at Stranraer harbour. The flag on her flag pole was flying at half mast, the gangway was lowered and in complete silence the coffin of Captain James Ferguson was slowly carried off by members of the harbour staff. Nine other coffins were also solemnly brought ashore and placed in waiting hearses.

On Tuesday, 3 February, Larne was to see the first of many funerals pass through the town. Hundreds of men women and children stood in silence as the corteges passed at half hourly intervals. This day was to see five such processions make their way to the cemeteries at Larne and Glynn. The following day was to see a further eight funerals wend their lonely way through the streets of the town.

On Thursday, 3 February, the first of many funerals took place in Stranraer. Prior to the funerals starting, a Sunderland seaplane, manufactured at the Wig Bay

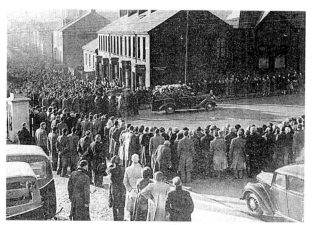

The funeral of Roseann Baxter turning up the Roddens in Larne. *Larne Times*

The funeral in Belfast of Major J Maynard Sinclair, Deputy Prime Minister of Northern Ireland. *Belfast Telegraph*

A detachment of men from HMS *Centaur* carry the remains of Chief Petty Officer Childs following a funeral service in Belfast. *Belfast Telegraph*

factory of Short Brothers and Harland, took off from the aircraft factory and flew to the position off the Copeland Islands where the *Princess Victoria* was lost. This particular aircraft was the last one to have been worked on by the majority of the Shorts' work force who had been lost.

Flight Lieutenant Ben Ford flew the aircraft and also on board was the Reverend AL Melrose from Stoneykirk. As the aeroplane reached the Copelands, the minister conducted a short service as wreaths were dropped into the Irish Sea. The Sunderland was met by a Sealand aeroplane which had flown from Belfast and both aeroplanes dropped to around 50 feet. As they flew over the spot where the ship had foundered they both dipped their wings in salute, before returning to their respective bases.

While this airborne tribute was being paid, the first of nine funerals took place in the *Princess Victoria*'s home port. Captain Ferguson had been buried on the previous day, his coffin borne by the crew of the Portpatrick lifeboat. The coffin of Radio Officer David Broadfoot was carried by officers from Portpatrick Radio station through the town of Stranraer. A wreath spelling the ship's call sign was placed on the coffin. The funeral of Chief Officer Shirley Duckels made its way to Inch for burial. The following day saw another three funerals make their way through the port.

In Belfast funerals were also taking place. Over 4,000 people lined the route that was taken by the cortege of Major J Maynard Sinclair as it proceeded to Lambeg. Lord Birkenhead represented the British government while the Prime Minister of Northern Ireland also attended.

The funeral in Stranraer of Captain James Ferguson.
*The Bulletin and Scots Pictorial*

Just 14 days after the loss of the ship, the Royal National Lifeboat Institution awarded Bronze medals for gallantry to William McConnell and Hugh Nelson, the coxswains of the Portpatrick and Donaghadee lifeboats. James Mitchell and James Armstrong, the engineers of the respective lifeboats, were presented with certificates acclaiming the thanks of the RNLI. These certificates, which are infrequently awarded, were inscribed in velum. Each crew member was awarded the sum of £5 and presented with an engraved pewter mug. The crew of the Cloughey lifeboat, which also launched on 31 January, were also presented with the £5 award.

In October 1953 it was announced that Honours would be presented to many of those whose lives were touched by the sinking of the *Princess Victoria*. Radio Officer David Broadfoot, who stayed at his post transmitting messages until the very end, was posthumously awarded the George Cross. During the voyage Broadfoot sent a total of 54 messages. Part of his citation read:

> Thinking only of saving the lives of passengers and crew, Radio Officer Broadfoot remained in his cabin receiving and sending messages, although he must have known that if he did this he would have no chance of surviving.

The award was presented by Queen Elizabeth II to Mrs May Broadfoot at Buckingham Palace on 2 October 1953.

It was further announced that the MBE would be presented to Captain James Alexander Bell, the master of the MV *Lairdsmoor*; David Brewster, skipper of the fishing trawler *Eastcoates*; Captain James Kelly of the *Pass of Drumochter*; and Captain Hugh Angus Matheson of the MV *Orchy*. These awards were in recognition of their attempts to rescue survivors.

The British Empire Medal (Civil Division) was awarded to William McConnell, coxswain of the Portpatrick lifeboat, and also to Hugh Nelson of the Donaghadee lifeboat for the part they played in the rescue.

Finally, the George Medal was awarded to two members of the crew of the HMS *Contest*. Lieutenant Commander Stanley Lawrence McArdle MVO RN and Chief Petty Officer Wilfred Warren received this award for the rescue of James Gilmore from a raft. Part of the citation stated: "The gallantry and presence of mind

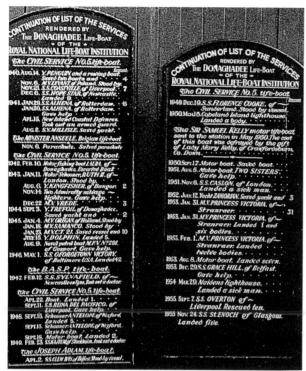

The role of honour of rescues by the Donaghadee lifeboat.
*Board of Governors, Bangor Grammar School*

The Princess Victoria Memorial as originally situated in the middle of Agnew Park, Stranraer.

*Whiteholme Publishers*

shown by Lt. Commander McArdle and C.P.O. Warren in the quite exceptional weather conditions undoubtedly saved the man's life."

Agnew Park, overlooking Loch Ryan and the port in Stranraer, was to be the setting for a memorial dedicated to those people from the Scottish town who lost their lives when the ship sank. The local council approached Mr Ian Macdonald, a chartered architect, and gave him the commission to design the memorial. In pursuing this task, Mr Macdonald felt that it should be a memorial which evoked what had happened, and should be so visually demanding that the passer-by would take those few extra steps to view it and remember the past events of the Scottish port. His design is in the shape of a Scottish burial cairn made from granite stone and is similar to the outline of Ailsa Craig, which seafarers would pass on their journey from Scotland to Northern Ireland. On top of the memorial is an anchor, representing the trust of seafarers in being held fast and also recalling that those who care will always hold fast to the memory of those lost.

A service of dedication was held on a sunny Sunday,

8 July 1962. Officials from the local council, including the Provost, Mr RE Caughie, paraded through the town to the park, where hundreds of people waited for the service. An area had been set aside for relatives of those who were lost.

Provost Caughie told those gathered that this day would bring back all the sad memories of that day in January 1953 when the tempest which had raged around the shores had caused death and destruction on a scale that few people would have experienced in peacetime. He said that many of the younger people present would only have vague recollections of the tragedy and it was fitting that the memorial should serve to instruct future generations about the loss of the gallant ship and those who sailed in her. He added that the simple rugged cairn, surmounted

Another view of the Scottish memorial, representing a Scottish burial cairn, as now situated at the entrance to Agnew Park, Stranraer. *Author's collection*

by an anchor, overlooking Loch Ryan fittingly symbolised the devotion to duty and steadfastness of those men and also the deep sorrow which the loss of so many lives had left in the community. He unveiled a bronze plaque attached to the Memorial which read:

On the morning of 31st January 1953, the MV Princess Victoria left the East pier Stranraer, to make its normal crossing to Larne. Off Corsewall Point, the ship encountered the full fury of the gale which was that day to cause so much damage and loss throughout the Country and, despite the valiant efforts of her crew, the lifeboatmen and other seafarers, the 'Princess Victoria' foundered off the coast of Northern Ireland with the loss of 133 lives, of those lost 23 were inhabitants of Stranraer, whose death this community mourns.

In the early 1990s a grant from the National Lottery was made available to the town of Stranraer in order to redevelop Agnew Park. A major outcry occurred when the memorial cairn was basically demolished, the plan

The dedication on the Scottish memorial, noting that 23 inhabitants of Stranraer died on the ship.    *Author's collection*

Construction work commencing on the Larne memorial, overlooking the harbour.            *Larne Borough Council*

being to relocate it. There were many letters to the local paper from residents of the town demanding that the memorial be reinstated. Eventually it was rebuilt using new stone and placed in its current location at the entrance to the park, tucked away behind trees and bushes and out of sight of Loch Ryan.

Early in 1979, at a meeting of Larne Borough Council, a proposal was raised to the effect that the town of Larne should have a memorial to the *Princess Victoria*. After several meetings it was finally agreed, on 24 September of the same year, that the proposal be adopted. The council minutes recorded the agreement: "To proceed with the work and site the memorial on the green area at the bottom of Bay Road." Larne Council sought quotations for the memorial and two tenders were received. DJ McKee of Glynn near Larne quoted £1,985 for a basalt stone memorial, while sculptor Dan McCaske from Ballymena quoted a costing of £2,500 for a granite memorial. The council chose the latter quotation and while publicly announcing their decision, asked for donations towards the memorial. By January over £1,600 had been raised by subscription from members of the public, business firms, churches, clubs and associations, shipping firms and the Larne Port Authority. The council decided to proceed and agreed they would provide the extra funds to supplement the public subscriptions. Work on the memorial started in early 1980 and was completed by September of the same year, when the memorial was unveiled. It is situated on the shore side of Bay Road in Larne, overlooking the shipping that passes in and out of the port. Constructed as a square granite pedestal, upon which rests a metal anchor, it carries a plaque on the front face, bearing the same wording as the Stranraer memorial

except to record that of the total of 133 lives lost, 27 were inhabitants of Larne.

Following the loss of the *Princess Victoria*, one organisation, the local Royal Antediluvian Order of Buffaloes, became actively involved in collecting funds for the memorial. Since it has been erected, the Order have held a religious service at the site each year on 31 January at 11.00 am. On each occasion, a different local clergyman has been invited to officiate at the short service which has over the years been attended by many of those local people affected by the sinking. Hopefully, the Royal Antediluvian Order of Buffaloes will continue to remember the loss of the ship, her passengers and crew for many years to come.

The completed memorial in Larne at Bay Road.

*Author's collection*

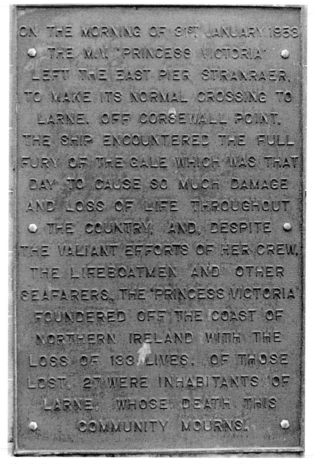

ON THE MORNING OF 31ST JANUARY 1953 THE M.V. "PRINCESS VICTORIA" LEFT THE EAST PIER STRANRAER, TO MAKE ITS NORMAL CROSSING TO LARNE. OFF CORSEWALL POINT, THE SHIP ENCOUNTERED THE FULL FURY OF THE GALE WHICH WAS THAT DAY TO CAUSE SO MUCH DAMAGE AND LOSS OF LIFE THROUGHOUT THE COUNTRY. AND, DESPITE THE VALIANT EFFORTS OF HER CREW, THE LIFEBOATMEN AND OTHER SEAFARERS, THE "PRINCESS VICTORIA" FOUNDERED OFF THE COAST OF NORTHERN IRELAND WITH THE LOSS OF 133 LIVES. OF THOSE LOST, 27 WERE INHABITANTS OF LARNE, WHOSE DEATH THIS COMMUNITY MOURNS.

The dedication on the Larne memorial noting that 27 inhabitants of the town were lost on the ship. *Author's collection*

# *Warnings of disaster*

When the *Princess Victoria* sailed from Stranraer on the last fateful voyage on 31 January 1953, the ship was almost six years old. Yet in that short period there had been four incidents that had occurred which should have had alarm bells ringing in the minds of the ship's manager and owners. However, they were later to claim that they were not fully aware of the full history of the ship.

Two of the incidents were of a minor nature and were the result of the ship colliding with the quayside. The other two occurrences, when large quantities of free-flowing milk and then sea water were on the car deck were of a more serious nature.

The first serious incident occurred on 25 November 1949 when the ship was crossing from Larne to Stranraer, with Captain Ferguson in charge. On the car deck were 16 milk tankers, with a weight of about 10 tons each and a capacity of between 1,500 and 2,000 gallons for each tanker. The weather was blowing a force 8–9 gale with the wind aft of the vessel. In these conditions the ship was rolling heavily and the tankers became loose, some starting to slide towards the port side of the car deck. Two of the tankers went over on their sides and the tanks broke free from their chassis, causing an immediate list of about 10 degrees.

Second Officer Leslie Unsworth came onto the car deck and decided that getting rid of the milk in the overturned tankers was his priority, which would hopefully reduce the list on the ship. He proceeded to open the valves on four of the tankers and allow the contents to drain onto the car deck. This then resulted in about 6,000 gallons of milk, to a depth in places of nine inches, flowing freely about on the car deck. With the list in the ship, sea water was also entering the car deck through the sliding doors in the side of the hull, forced in by the pressure of the sea. The resulting mixture of sea water and milk managed to drain into the engine room of the ship. Clearly this was a most dangerous and precarious position to be in. To add to Unsworth's problems, petrol was also flowing onto the car deck, having escaped from the vehicles' petrol tanks. The rear guillotine door had been lowered before the ship set sail from Larne, adding some extra strength to the rear

doors. Crew members using brooms were immediately ordered to sweep the mixture of water, milk and petrol towards the scuppers, which took well over 40 minutes to clear from the car deck. Unsworth stated that he later told Mr AL Finlayson, a ships' surveyor for the Ministry of Transport, about the incident, and he would also have kept Captain Ferguson aware of what was happening during that crossing.

The second incident involving the *Princess Victoria* occurred on 20 September 1950, when she was berthing at the railway pier at Stranraer at about 11.25 in the morning. The day was cloudy, with a fresh to strong west-south-west wind blowing, but visibility was good. The ship failed to pull up in time and the stern of the vessel struck the ramp causing minor damage to the hull and superstructure. Both engines were going full speed ahead to slow the ship down as she reversed towards the pier. Captain Ferguson was in charge, assisted by Chief Officer Duckels. On this occasion only minor damage was caused and there was no report of any damage caused to the stern doors. However, Jack Adamson, who was the pantryman on the ship that day, recalls that the vessel was reversing rather quickly and the collision with the pier resulted in quite a few people in the lounge falling over. After the ship was docked he went to the car deck to see what had happened. Jack later recalled that there had been quite a bit of damage caused to the wooden ramp on the quayside. With regard to the incident, the log for the *Princess Victoria* states:

At 11.24 at Stranraer

When berthing stern first at 11.24 hours today at the Railway Pier, Stranraer Harbour, vessel did not pull up in time with the result the stern came in contact with the Ramp berth at our stern. Both engines were going full speed ahead at the time of the incident.

Superficial damage was caused to the shell plating and superstructure about the waterline at stern of the vessel. Cloudy clear weather with Fresh to Strong WSW wind when berthing.

Signed S. Duckels Chief Officer, J.M. Ferguson, Master

The third incident again resulted in large quantities of water coming onto the car deck. In fact, what happened in the early hours of Sunday morning, 25 November 1951 should have been a major warning to the captain, crew and owners of the potential for a further serious accident to occur. The ship was under the command of acting Captain Shirley Duckels, with John Hey as the acting chief officer. The *Princess Victoria* was attempting to enter Larne harbour, having left Stranraer at 23.30 on the previous evening. As the ship approached the Maidens, on the approach to Larne, a strong wind blew up from the north-east. This quite quickly developed into hurricane force at the same time as the ship was starting to turn around to begin its approach, stern first, into Larne harbour. The vessel would not respond. Duckels tried to take her into the wind, stern first, to bring her round to enter Larne, but as the stern came into the wind and the sea, the vessel shipped a heavy sea straight into the car deck. The time was about 01.25. The ship immediately took on a list of about 10 degrees to starboard.

The captain decided that he could not attempt to berth in the strong wind without causing a further hazard for the ship, so he set course for Stranraer. Hey was sent to the car deck to investigate. What met him was water to a depth of three feet at the starboard side of the car deck, with the level amidships about one and a half to to two feet. It was estimated that between 75 to 100 tons of water had breached the doors and was now on the car deck. This figure of 100 tons, or approximately 22,000 gallons, was about half of the quantity of water that was shipped on the fateful crossing on 31 January 1953. On further investigation, Hey discovered that the rear stern doors had been buckled by the sea, with the starboard door opened to the sea. The door itself was not damaged, but the bolts and securing stays were. Using crowbars, the crew was able to close it over and managed to secure it. The ship continued on its course back to Stranraer with this water discharging through the scuppers on the car deck. The journey lasted until 05.30, some three and half hours after the doors were breached. It was to take a full hour and a half for all the water to clear from the deck.

Surprisingly the ship proceeded on with two complete crossings before the locking bolts and stays were replaced and new ones fitted at a cost of just £10 by WH Kane of Larne. The following day, Duckels wrote a letter to Captain Harry Perry, the marine superintendent of British Railways, giving details of the incident. To safeguard himself, Duckels also sent a copy of the letter to a firm of solicitors in Stranraer, Messrs Foster and Ferguson. In the letter, which was dated 26 November 1951, Duckels stated:

> The stern doors of this ship (The Princess Victoria) were buckled and some pins bent on Sunday 25 November at approx. 01.50 off the entrance to Loch Larne. The damage occurred in the second of two attempts to enter the harbour in stormy weather.
>
> Some water was shipped into the car deck and subsequently cleared through scuppers while the ship proceeded at slow speed.
>
> The Princess Victoria left Stranraer at 23.31 on 24/11/51 in calm weather. A freshening NE wind at 01.20 25/11/51 quickly became a NE gale with fierce squalls and a very rough sea.
>
> The ship returned to Loch Ryan and brought to anchor at 05.30 25/11. The damage to the stern doors did not delay the landing and loading of milk tankers.
>
> Temporary repairs will be made as quickly as possible.

The final incident with the *Princess Victoria* was not the fault of anyone connected with the ship. On 2 November 1952 the vessel was tied up at the mail berth in Larne harbour when she was struck on the starboard side by the SS *Empire Gaelic*, which was leaving Larne bound for Preston. The resulting collision resulted in the forward moorings of the *Princess Victoria* being carried away and with the *Empire Gaelic* lying across her bows she drifted backwards and struck the pier and ramp with her stern. The *Princess Victoria* was later taken out of service and sailed to Henderson's shipyard in Glasgow, where she stayed for four days. On examination it was discovered that apart from the damage to the bow and hull of the ship, the guide rails of the rear guillotine door, which would come down over the stern doors, were also damaged. This meant that the sliding guillotine door could still be moved up and down but would not fully cover and lock onto the stern doors, as it had originally been designed to do. The ship surveyor recommended that the damage to the guillotine door could be rectified at the owners' convenience. The *Princess Victoria* was then put back into service.

Had the crew and owners paid more attention to these incidents, and understood the phenomenon of a condition now referred to as the 'free surface effect of water', the *Princess Victoria* might not have been lost.

# The Inquiry
## 11

The Minister of Transport, Mr Alan Lennox-Boyd, announced at Westminster on Friday, 13 February that an Inquiry would be held into the loss of the *Princess Victoria*, under the terms of the Merchant Shipping Act 1894. The setting for the Inquiry was to be the Crumlin Road Courthouse in Belfast.

A week later in Dáil Éireann in Dublin, Mr MacBride TD asked Mr Sean Lemass, the Minister for Industry and Commerce, if in his view the Irish government should be represented at the forthcoming Inquiry. Mr MacBride further asked the Minister to consider the current provision of rescue facilities in the Irish Sea should such a crisis reoccur. Mr Lemass replied that the vessel was owned and registered in Britain, and that on publication of the findings of the Court, the outcome would be generally available. He concluded by stating that if 'we' ( the Irish government) were holding a public inquiry in respect of a vessel owned and registered in Ireland, he did not think that the Irish government would look favourably on a request by the British government to be represented.

The chairman of the Inquiry was to be Mr John H Campbell QC RM, and his three assessors were to be Captain CV Groves of Ipswich; Professor AM Robb Dsc MINA of Glasgow University; and Mr J Shand, a marine engineer from Glasgow. Mr George Courtney, who was the chief clerk to the petty sessions in Belfast, was appointed as clerk of the court.

The Ministry of Transport set the Inquiry a total 48 questions that it wished answered in relation to the ship and the circumstances surrounding her loss.

Mr Campbell and his assessors sat for their first day of evidence on 23 March 1953. In total, 66 witnesses were to be called to give evidence during 22 days of examination. Those taking part comprised five Queen's Counsellors and 17 barristers representing the Ministry of Transport; the ship's owners, the British Transport Commission; the ship's builders, William Denny and Brothers Ltd; the master and officers of the ship; the National Union of Seamen and various other unions; Lloyd's Register of Shipping; the Royal National Lifeboat Institution; and

Mr John H Campbell QC RM, chairman of the *Princess Victoria* Inquiry that was held at the Courthouse on the Crumlin Road, Belfast.          *M Campbell collection*

Mr George Courtney, clerk to the Inquiry, with his secretary, compiling the report.          *S Herron collection*

relatives of those lost.

On the first day of the Inquiry, 23 March, the court was supplied with a large-scale replica model of the *Princess Victoria* and a working model of the stern doors of the ship. Three witnesses were called that day to give evidence. The first two – William Pirrie, the dock foreman, and Donald McGregor, the Harbour Master – were both from the port of Stranraer. Pirrie told of how he had come on duty at just after midnight on the Saturday morning and supervised the loading of the cargo onto the *Princess Victoria*. McGregor gave the court details of the cargo that was carried by the ship that morning and also furnished details of how the cargo was generally loaded. He stated that the method of loading involved the cargo being lifted aboard by the dockside steam crane on a wooden tray. These trays were then lowered onto a four-wheel barrow which was towed along the deck by a Lister motor tractor to the required position. The goods were taken out of the tray and stowed on wooden trays on deck. The *Princess Victoria* was supplied with 40 of these trays. When the ship sailed, the motor tractor was generally taken on the crossing. The trays, McGregor said, were placed hard against a wooden ramp that kept the cargo clear of the scuppers. He added that the cargo could not block the scuppers as they were protected by a beam a foot high

running in front of them. He also made reference to the fact that two cars that were to be transported on that voyage could not be loaded due to strong winds making the quayside crane inoperable. McGregor added that he could only remember that happening on two previous occasions.

The final witness of the first day was Robert Hay, a principal scientific officer with the Meteorological Office of the Air Ministry. He spent some considerable time explaining and deciphering the various weather reports that had been submitted as evidence from a variety of weather stations – West Freugh RAF station, south of Stranraer; Portpatrick; the BBC; and the Northern Ireland weather station. In his evidence he stated that at noon on the day in question the sea in the North Channel would have produced waves of 23 feet (7 metres), and at 3.00 pm waves of 26 feet (7.92 metres). Questioned by Mr JB Hewson for the British Transport Commission, Hay stated that with a combination of high winds, a cross-tide running and heavy seas being pushed against a shelving shore at the entrance to Loch Ryan, his estimate of wave height may have been less that was actually experienced.

Day two of the Inquiry was to see three crew members who survived give evidence. Angus Nelson, an able seaman, told the court how he had been at sea for 29 years and served on the *Princess Victoria* since the ship came

Members of the crew of the *Princess Victoria* pictured outside Crumlin Road Courthouse prior to giving evidence to the Inquiry. Left to right, Angus Nelson, James Clements, Malcolm McKinnon, Thomas McQuiston and Alexander Craig.     *J Thompson collection*

into service in 1947. He explained to the Inquiry that when the ship was at the mouth of Lough Ryan he had been ordered to go forward to the forecastle with other crew members to try to release the bow rudder. Nelson stated that due to the heavy sea, and waves crashing over the bow, they were unable to release the locking mechanism. Asked about the rear guillotine door, Nelson replied: "The only occasion I saw it down was at Dumbarton when it was fitted . . . It was not in use since."

Thomas McQuiston, the cargoman, was the next witness to give evidence. He stated that he had served on the ship since January 1953 and that his main duties were to check the cargo on board and ensure that it was stowed properly. Prior to sailing he was accompanied by Chief Officer Shirley Duckels. Both of them checked and closed the sliding side doors of the ship, through which the cargo had been loaded. He informed the court that he had witnessed the initial wave breaching the stern doors as he was on the car deck adjacent to the turntable. The first wave, he recounted, travelled the full length of the car deck and hit him where he stood. Asked about the rear doors, McQuiston stated that since he had joined the ship only 30 days before it sank, he was not really that familiar with their operation. He added that during his period of service, especially while the ship was loading at Stranraer, he had never seen the stern doors open, nor had he seen the guillotine door ever lowered over them. The chairman, Mr Campbell, asked, "Did it not strike you as extraordinary that this door was never down?" McQuiston replied, "I didn't know what it was really for. I thought it might be lowered in rough weather or something like that." Mr Campbell then asked, "Did you never ask anyone why it was not down?" The reply was terse: "It was no business of mine." McQuiston informed the court that the crew had done their duty throughout the emergency.

Malcolm McKinnon was the last witness to give evidence that day, continuing the following day, as well as being recalled to give further evidence on 30 March – the sixth day. McKinnon, who had served on the *Princess Victoria* for four and a half years and been at sea since November 1938, told the court that as the ship left Stranraer "there was a gale blowing, but nothing out of the ordinary". He recalled how he had been standing at the galley door and saw the sea burst over the ship, coming as far forward as where he was standing. He was one of the seamen who were told to go down to the car deck to try and repair the stern doors. Under questioning he said:

> There was not much that we could do, because the door was damaged. It would have endangered life to try to close it. We got it closed about one third of the way and then had to leave it alone because we could not do anything with it.

Mr McSparran QC, representing the Amalgamated Transport and General Workers Union, pressed McKinnon regarding the scuppers on the car deck. His reply was that the deck scuppers did not clear water as quickly as he would have wished.

On the third day of the Inquiry the court convened as normal at 10.30, but adjourned for half an hour as a mark of respect for the death of Queen Mary, who had passed away earlier that morning.

Malcolm McKinnon was the first witness of the day. The chairman asked him, "Would the ship still be afloat if the stern doors had held?" McKinnon replied, "I hardly think so." In further evidence McKinnon explained that as the crew were attempting to close the doors, the sea was breaking over the starboard quarter and running down into the car deck. There was, he stated, more water getting into the ship than there was getting out of it.

Lieutenant Commander Harvey Fleming, captain of HMS *Contest*, told the court of how they had been moored at Rothesay Bay and had received instructions to proceed to the assistance of the *Princess Victoria* at 10.26 am. His was the only vessel engaged in the rescue that could communicate directly with the ship. He explained that obviously the location of the ship kept changing and they were continually altering their course to compensate. HMS *Contest* did not arrive at the last known position until 3.00 pm. Asked by Mr Topping QC, representing the Ministry of Transport, if he had known the exact position where the ship was to sink and had made directly for it from Rothesay, would he have got there before the loss. Fleming answered, "No." He also explained to the court how his crew rescued several men from life rafts, and then took them to Belfast.

John Garrett, an able seaman, was the final witness of the day and he recalled to the Inquiry how he had been ordered down to the car deck to assist in the attempt to close the stern doors. Both the port and the starboard doors were stove in and there was already about two feet of sea water on the deck when he arrived. Mr McSparran QC, representing several of the unions, asked if the doors were stove outwards. Garrett replied that they had been forced inwards.

Four witnesses were called on the fourth day: James Blair, a steward on the ship; David Brewster, the master of one of the rescue vessels, the MV *Eastcoates*; John Murdoch, an able seaman; and Charles Thompson, an assistant steward.

Brewster told the court how he had been the skipper of fishing trawlers for 30 years, and how he had left Fleetwood the day previous to the disaster, only to encounter heavy seas, and made for the shelter of Belfast Lough. He stated that because of the bad weather he kept his radio switched on and he relayed details to the court of the first distress messages that he picked up, including one regarding the fishing vessel *Michael Griffith* (her captain was a close friend of Brewster). As his vessel was so far away from Corsewall Point and other vessels reported being nearer, Brewster took the decision not to try to cross the North Channel. When it became obvious that the *Princess Victoria*'s actual position was closer to the Copeland Islands, he immediately set sail to assist. He was to give the court some harrowing evidence regarding the lifebelts on the bodies that he recovered. Asked if all the people in the water were wearing life jackets, he replied:

> Quite a lot of them were, and a lot had been choked in jumping into the water. I understand that quite a lot of people had to jump off the ship, I am sure that if anybody jumped from any distance at all into the water, these things would have come up and choked them straight away. The survivor we picked up was semi-conscious when we got him on board. Before we got him he was pulling his life jacket down from his neck. He must have known that if he let the lifebelt go, he would have choked.

When telling the court of the rescue, Brewster could not recall the exact time he arrived at the position near the Copeland Islands. Mr Topping QC, representing the Ministry of Transport, pressed Brewster on this point. The latter's reply – "It took me all my time to look after the darn ship, never mind the times" – showed his frustration at the question. The chairman, Mr Campbell, then told Brewster, "It is the unanimous opinion of this court, Mr Brewster, that your conduct on the occasion is worthy of the highest

praise." Mr Topping quickly stated that he agreed with the chairman's comments.

Able Seaman John Murdoch told the court how he was in the forward lounge when the ship was hit by the waves and opened the door to have a look into the car deck. He then closed the door and assisted in the unsuccessful attempt to close the stern doors. He told Mr Nicholson, QC for the Transport Commission, that he felt the scuppers were useless, as the cargo had been swept over them and it was impossible for anyone to clear them. The chairman then asked Murdoch about emergency boat stations and was told that the only order he knew about was lining up on deck as a member of the ship's boat crews. Mr Campbell asked him, "Were you not told how passengers should be assembled in an emergency?" Murdoch replied, "No."

James Blair, a steward, told how he was in the lounge when the sea hit the ship and how he and other passengers, including Maynard Sinclair, were thrown towards the starboard side of the ship. During questioning, Blair was handed the model of the *Princess Victoria* and turned it on its side showing the amount of list that there was in the ship. He stated:

> Quite a few people jumped over the port side, but others did not jump, and stayed where they were at the port rail. The ship just whisked away from below them. It was possible to jump from the port side out over the bottom of the ship. . . I climbed over to the port rail at the bridge just below where Captain Ferguson was standing.

Assistant Steward Charles Thompson told the court how he had served early morning tea to the passengers who were still in their cabins, as the ship set sail. He then went and had his own breakfast in the third class dining saloon. He told how he assisted passengers to don their life jackets and help them make their way up to the deck. Thompson stated that when he issued the life jackets, the crew were instructed to tell passengers to hold them down as they entered the water. Mr Lowry, representing the Ministry of Transport, asked him, "What were you told the danger was if that precaution was not taken?" Thompson replied, "You might get your neck broken or something like that."

The fifth day of the Inquiry was to see the first of the surviving passengers give their account of their survival. Captain James Kerr, while a passenger on the ship, was an experienced seafarer who had travelled the waters of the Irish Sea. As such, his account of the events would be of immense interest and benefit to those present at the Inquiry. He informed the court that near the end he had overheard the captain ask an engineer with regard to the engines, "Can you give her a jag? After all, we are quite close to land." According to Kerr, the engineer told the captain that he was sorry but the engine room was flooded and he could do nothing. Mr Hanna, QC for next of kin of the officers and master, asked Captain Kerr if he had any knowledge how David Broadfoot, the radio operator, managed to remain at his post and continue to operate the equipment. Kerr replied, "He must have been hanging on like a fly on a window pane." He was also asked if he would have gone to sea on that day. He replied, "I certainly would have gone on. There was a moderate gale of wind blowing, but it was quite perfect and in order to go on."

The remainder of the day's evidence was given over to passenger William Copley and pantry boy William McAllister. Copley told the court how he went around the cabins on C deck to waken the passengers, coming across Sir Walter Smiles who was dressed in just his shirt and trousers. He recalled that after the ship had sank, he managed to get onto a raft on which there was also a woman, a young boy and a steward and that he was the only one who was able to hang on. William McAllister told of witnessing an attempt by some stewards to open the door from the lounge to the car deck, an extremely difficult task due to the amount of water behind the door on the car deck. He also recalled that when the ship was first hit by

William McAllister, John Stanford and James Blair arriving at Crumlin Road Courthouse to give evidence. *Belfast News Letter*

the heavy seas, a huge wave came over the starboard side and smashed against the galley window.

The sixth day was to see six witnesses called to give evidence: Donal McAteer, John Beer, James Clements, Alexander Craig, James Kelly and Malcolm McKinnon.

Petty Officer John Beer was asked if he had any difficulty with his life jacket; he replied, "No." Mr McGonigal, QC for the Transport and General Workers Union, asked him about the wave that he saw hitting the rear stern doors. Beer replied that no waves broke over the doors, but the waves did hit the rear doors exceptionally hard. He also added that as a sailor, he would not have expected a wave to have hit the ship in relation to the direction they were travelling. Crew members James Clements and Alexander Craig recalled their individual actions on the ship. Clements told of being in a lifeboat when the ship was sinking and how it turned completely over on itself and then landed right side up in the water, but that the boat's equipment fell out during the incident. Alexander Craig told of his attempt to close the open stern doors. After their efforts failed, he said that the doors were simply left lying open, with the sea coming in all the time.

James Kelly, the captain of the *Pass of Drumochter*, told how his ship became involved in the rescue, and how the only thing that he was really able to do was to provide some shelter from the waves for the lifeboats that he came across. Mr Campbell thanked him for the part he played in the rescue of the survivors.

The Inquiry did not sit until 11.00 am the following day, 31 March, as a mark of respect for the funeral of Queen Mary which was taking place in London.

In his evidence, William McConnell, coxswain of the Portpatrick lifeboat, stated that they were the first rescue vessel to respond to the assistance call, but the last to actually get there. McConnell also stated that if the *Princess Victoria* had had radio telephone communications instead of Morse, he felt that it would have made the task of locating the ship much easier. He said that it was normal practice for the Coastguard to set a course for the lifeboat, but that on this occasion he was being directed mainly by information relayed from the stricken ship, and that he would have needed the use of a chart. The chairman pursued this point by asking, "You carry charts. Why didn't you use them?" McConnell started to answer, "Well, on a normal day . . . " when the chairman interrupted, "But you are not called out on a normal day." The reply was, "On that day you couldn't walk on the deck. You could use the charts if you could get to the cabin."

William McGregor, the officer in charge of Portpatrick Radio station, was then called to give evidence. (He would be recalled to give further evidence on the last day of the Inquiry.) Mr Hanna QC, representing the Mercantile Marine Service Association, began the encounter:

Q. You let Captain Ferguson, charged with 180 lives, go on down, assuming you were taking information he was giving you, Mr McGregor and acting on it.

A. Well we did give him our bearing at 12.06.

Q. You withheld from the lifeboat the information which the Master of the ship had given you.

A. It had not been sent to him.

Q. On the 31st January shortly after 10.30 the Princess Victoria sent out a message SOS.

A. Yes.

Q. That is a most serious message for the master of any ship to send.

A. Yes, it is most serious.

Q. Around 14.00 hours, just 3½ hours later, the Princess Victoria sank?

A. Yes.

Q. With the loss of over 130 lives?

A. Yes.

Q. And no person on rescue operations saw the ship although it was within ten square miles, is that not so?

A. Yes.

Q. And still three months later there is no change in the operation?

A. I am afraid I cannot give you any further information.

William Spreadborough, the district officer of HM Coastguard at Portpatrick, was also, like McGregor, called to give evidence on two occasions, on this day and also the last day. He too was to be probed about his actions on the day of the disaster. Under questioning from Mr Fox for the National Union of Seamen, he stated that when the SOS was received from the ship the Coastguard were relying on the positions given to them by the *Princess Victoria*. They found that they did not know the exact location of the vessel and that it was not until sometime after 1.00 pm that it was fully realised that the ship was under her own power and at the mercy of wind and sea. He did not, in his opinion, place any great reliance on the bearing from Seaforth, but it later transpired that this was an accurate bearing. At the end of his evidence the chairman, Mr Campbell, said to Spreadborough that he and his fellow assessors at the Inquiry were of the opinion that he had done all he could and had done his job well.

James Bell, the captain of the *Lairdsmoor*, stated in his evidence that at around 2.40 pm he saw a shadow on his radar screen which then became an echo and stayed there for about two minutes. He was asked if this could have been the *Princess Victoria* sinking. He replied, "I do not know, I would not like to say."

Wednesday, 1 April, saw William McConnell, the coxswain of the Portpatrick lifeboat, recalled as the first witness of the day. Mr Campbell referred McConnell to evidence that he had given on the previous day when he was asked if he was the coxswain of the lifeboat and he replied, "I was." The chairman then asked what he meant by that reply. McConnell replied that he had resigned from the position prior to the sinking of the ship. Mr Campbell asked him his reason for this and McConnell stated that he would rather not answer the question, which was accepted by the chairman. This seems rather odd, that in an official inquiry McConnell was permitted not to give a full answer.

Passenger Frederick Baird recalled in his evidence the last few moments of the ship and how the passengers had to look after themselves. As far as he could see, there was no help for the women and children when they had to climb over the rails, as the ship was turning over.

Hugh Nelson, the coxswain of the Donaghadee lifeboat, told of his crew's efforts in the rescue bid. He stated that they left Donaghadee virtually blind, knowing only that the ship was in distress between Portpatrick and Belfast. He did state that if he had known the position of the ship, he could have been with the *Princess Victoria* within an hour of setting sail, and possibly have been there in the period immediately after the ship had sunk.

Captain Samuel Iles of the *Princess Margaret* was questioned at length about his opinion on whether the ship should have sailed on that day. He said that the final decision was the captain's and that in his experience there had never been a sailing cancelled from Stranraer. He informed the court that his ship had six freeing ports fitted in addition to the scuppers and that the lifeboat davits on the *Princess Margaret* were different, in that they all had to be screwed out by hand and were not the gravity type as fitted on the *Princess Victoria*. He was asked by Mr Massey, a solicitor for the relatives of David Broadfoot, about the position of the radio operator. Iles said that the door to the radio cabin was on the starboard side of the ship and that when the ship was on her side, the only way out would have been to jump straight down into the water. There would have been the possibility of David Broadfoot hitting the ship as he went down the deck. Mr Massey suggested that Broadfoot would have known that he was practically trapped in the cabin, to which Iles replied, "I do not see how he could have thought anything else." Iles also commented on a newspaper article by a Mr Hall, the late chief engineer of the ship, who stated that in his (Hall's) opinion, the first rough sea encountered by the *Princess Victoria* would finish the stern doors. He was further questioned about an article published in *The Spectator*, and written by 'Janus', which was also critical of the design of the stern doors.

The court then adjourned for Easter. During this period, counsel for the various groups represented were to take stock of how the Inquiry was proceeding for their respective clients. Queen's Counsel representing William Denny, the ship's builder, was concerned about the way the Inquiry was proceeding. One QC felt the evidence given in court to date was persuading the court and its chairman that the stern doors had not been of a suitable design for use in the North Channel. The same Counsel thought that the court may be reluctant to make a finding against the construction of the ship. Such a finding, he stated, would not be to the credit of British shipbuilding; indeed, it would be disastrous for the shipbuilder to be blamed for building a ship with a possible design fault. He was also concerned that if the finding of the court went against the builders and also British Railways, a liability of something in the region of £300,000 could be faced. Conveying his opinion, he believed the correct course of action would be "to lie as low as possible and to seek to attract the minimum of attention to ourselves". He was also extremely concerned about the evidence of Mr John D Hey, an ex-chief engineer on the *Princess Victoria*. He felt that Hey's evidence would make it abundantly clear that any weakness in the stern doors should have been apparent after 24 November 1951. His view was that they would be better leaving this witness alone. Hey had first-hand knowledge of the ship and the previous incidents when water was taken onto the car deck. In his original statement he said that an empty cigarette packet would have been capable of blocking a scupper. Obviously the learned QC did not wish to risk Hey giving detailed evidence of this nature to the Inquiry.

Following the nine-day break for the holidays, the court resumed and the first witness to be called was John D Hey. He was one of six witnesses called that day and his evidence, not surprisingly, was given rather quickly. He was asked about the incident when the ship took in water on the car deck, reversing into Larne harbour. He said that the cause for this was the ship going full astern on both engines on a 'big sea'. He stated that, in his opinion, an empty cigarette packet could easily block the scuppers.

William Millar, who had previously served as a second engineer on the ship, gave evidence about the construction and conditions in the engine room. He said that the door from the car deck to the engine room was not watertight, and added that the engines would keep running until there was at least six feet of water in that compartment. Asked how that amount of water could get into the engine room, Millar replied that he could not say. The chairman asked him if this was going to be one of the unsolved mysteries of the Inquiry, to which Millar replied, "As far as I am concerned."

That day also saw Captains Hugh Matheson of the MV *Orchy* and Malcolm Anderson of the rescue tug *Salveda* give evidence and recall their part in the rescue.

The court continued to sit the following day, a Saturday, and took evidence from Peter Hoare, Leslie Unsworth and John Reed. Commander Peter Hoare was the staff officer at the Maritime Headquarters at Pitreavie in Scotland. He explained to the court that the initial message he received regarding the *Princess Victoria* did not arrive with him until 10.22 am, at which point he had HMS *Contest* dispatched. He added that there had been several distress messages received that morning and that there was a system of priority, according to the messages received.

Hoare said that based on the information he had received, the situation with the *Princess Victoria* would not merit deployment of an aircraft. It was not until late in the afternoon that it was finally realised how serious the situation was. However, he added that a US Air Force aeroplane and several civil aircraft were told to keep a lookout for the ship.

Leslie Unsworth who had been the second officer on the ship from her commissioning until 1952, now gave evidence. He was asked about the incident in November 1949 when the milk tankers overturned. Unsworth informed the court of how two of the tankers full of milk had broken away from the chassis. He told how he released the milk from these and two other tankers on to the car deck, the milk flowing mostly to the fore end of the deck, with a depth of about nine inches extending aft to the position of the turntable. Unsworth further informed the court that there would have been about 6,000 gallons of milk mixing with the petrol, which had also spilled from the vehicle fuel tanks, and sea water. This mixture took 45 minutes to clear from the deck, the engineers complaining that some of it found its way down to the engine room.

Unsworth was asked by Mr McSparran QC if he would have considered it beyond the human mind to imagine a force 12 gale in the North Channel, to which he replied, "Until this one I would not have anticipated it." He also stated that he had informed Mr Finlayson, a ships' surveyor, about the incident in November 1951 when water entered through the rear stern doors while trying to enter Larne harbour.

Captain James Reed was the next witness to be called and he was to give evidence for two days. Reed informed the court that he had been appointed as the designated manager for the *Princess Victoria* in January 1952 and that she was one of 25 ships under his control. He stated that he had the fullest confidence in Captain Ferguson and Chief Officer Duckels. Under questioning, he informed the court that an application had been made to allow the *Princess Victoria* to ply the Harwich–Hook of Holland route, but this was turned down because the ship did not have large enough scuppers or enough freeing ports to drain the car deck. Reed was asked if he was aware of the two previous incidents when water had entered the car deck. He replied, "I was not." He added that these incidents occurred before he took over as the manager. On assuming the position, he

was given 50–80 files regarding the *Princess Victoria*, each containing 100–200 letters. He added:

> There was nothing in those files to give rise to any anxiety in connection with the continuing operating of the vessel, the protest letter [written by Duckels] if I had seen it would not give cause for concern, as all ships take water. There was nothing whatsoever in the 1951 incident to give any cause for concern.

On his second day of giving evidence, Captain Reed stated that even though the car deck was seven feet above the sea, and that there was water on it, he considered it beyond a possibility for a vessel to have shipped water as she did on the day of the disaster. Mr Campbell, the chairman, engaged Reed on the subject of the scuppers on the ship. Reed stated that during his four visits to the ship in 1952 no officer had ever voiced any complaint about the scuppers. Referring to the milk tanker incident, Mr Campbell asked Reed to give him an explanation of why he had never heard about it. Reed replied, "I do not know." The chairman then made the comment that he felt Reed was delegating a lot of his authority and that in his opinion there was a lot of 'flabby management' involved.

Flying Officer George Owen, the captain of the RAF Hastings aircraft, then gave evidence and described how he took off from Aldergrove Airport to proceed to Corsewall Point and was then diverted to the Copeland Islands. He said that his aircraft was equipped with radar and that if an aircraft had been in the area two hours earlier, radar could have been used to pinpoint the location of the ship.

The day's evidence concluded with Captain Harry Perry, the Marine Superintendent for British Railways. He informed the court that he had been the manager of the ship prior to Captain Reed taking over the post. He said that at no time while he was the manager did he ever receive any complaints about the ship's seaworthiness.

Captain Perry continued to give evidence on the Monday, 13 April, the eleventh day of the Inquiry. He informed the court that the weather reports were taken by the radio operator prior to the ship sailing and then passed to the captain. He again stressed that he had had no knowledge of the previous incidents, when sea water entered the car deck. Under examination from Mr McSparran, Perry stated that even if the stern doors of the ship had buckled in bad weather and shipped water through them, he would consider that the vessel was in no danger of shipping heavy seas through the stern doors in a force 12 gale. He never considered that there was a danger to the ship in the confused seas off Corsewall Point. Perry also said the disaster occurred because of phenomenal weather, and that "the *Princess Victoria* was a marvellous little boat".

The chief draughtsman of William Denny, Elmer Cotton, then began his evidence which lasted for three days. In a lengthy examination and cross-examination, Cotton was asked if he contemplated that the scuppers would have to free the car deck of large quantities of water, to which he replied, "We did not." He commented that the scuppers were designed to remove only the amount of water that would be required to wash down the deck. Cotton also stated that the design of the ship was a combination of responsibility between the builders, the owners, the Ministry of Transport and Lloyd's. On the subject of the stern doors, he stated that plans were submitted to the owners for approval. There was nothing in the ship's specification dealing with their strength or the fastenings which were to be used.

The following day Cotton was extensively questioned about the ship's design, including the lifeboat davits; the ventilation to the engine room; the connecting door between the car deck and the lounge; the life rafts; and the rear guillotine door. At the end of his evidence, Mr Campbell asked Cotton, "If reinforced doors had been fitted . . . would they have withstood the seas of January 31?" Cotton replied, "There is no doubt that they would have withstood the seas."

Passenger James Carlin was recalled and was asked about his attempt to rescue his wife, her mother and sister. After giving his evidence, the chairman thanked him for his contribution in what must have been very trying circumstances and passed on the sympathy of the court.

The fourteenth day of the Inquiry opened on 15 April with Elmer Cotton finishing evidence to the court.

Alfred Wilmott, the captain of the Belfast–Heysham ferry the *Duke of Argyll*, gave evidence on how he became aware of the disaster and the request for him to take his ferry to the aid of the *Princess Victoria*. He stated that his ship was berthed in Belfast and that the crew had left. It would have taken nearly three hours to reach the scene and his ship would not have been of much benefit in the rescue attempt.

Captain William Morrow, an assistant general manager with British Railways, also gave evidence. He stated that in August 1952, whilst on the car deck of the *Princess Victoria*, he had had a conversation with Captain Ferguson as milk tankers were being loaded. According to Morrow, Ferguson said, "It might be a good idea if we had bigger scuppers here." They were standing by the starboard engine room door at the time. The main reason for Captain Ferguson's statement, Morrow said, was that passengers would get their feet wet on the deck when going to their cars. He did not consider the matter to be urgent, and pointed out that it took him seven months to find out the full story about the previous flooding of the car deck. Morrow said that he felt no one on the ship attached any great importance to the shipping of water on the car deck. Mr McSparran QC asked if the ship should have been designed to cope with the type of weather that she met when the stern doors gave way. Morrow replied, "She was." He denied that British Railways were so proud of the ship that they may have been blind to any possible faults.

The day also saw evidence given by two marine engineers from British Railways – Thomas Copland and John Gibson – who told the court of the various inspections that they had undertaken. James Clark, a principal surveyor for Lloyd's Register of Shipping, also gave evidence about the strength of the ship.

The sixteenth day of the Inquiry was to hear detailed technical evidence from six ship surveyors regarding the ship and how she was inspected.

Alexander Aitken, a surveyor from Lloyd's, told of 122 visits to the ship during construction. He recommended that the ship be classed "+A with freeboard for Irish Channel Service", although he had never sailed on the Irish Sea. He too stated that he did not anticipate water coming over the top of the doors. Under questioning, Aitken agreed that water would have cleared more freely from the car deck if the ship had been fitted with freeing ports in addition to the scuppers.

Sydney Bryden, a principal surveyor for Lloyd's, stated that a sea could not be shipped on the car deck because the *Princess Victoria* was on a restricted service within easy reach of a port or refuge, on both sides of the channel. It would be possible for her to leave port in abnormal weather and the ship also had 150% more reserve buoyancy than required. The scuppers were considered to be primarily intended for drainage purposes and were adequate to deal with the amount of water that might enter the car deck.

Angus Finlayson, a surveyor for the Ministry of Transport, was asked about a conversation he had had with Leslie Unsworth regarding the shipping of water while reversing into Larne. He stated that he felt it would have been a considerable asset to have had additional freeing arrangements in the open bridge space. He reported this to his headquarters, but did not consider that the access of such water was a danger to the integrity of the ship. Finlayson denied that he was ever told that the aft doors had also buckled.

John Maxwell, the British Railways clerk at Stranraer, told of his efforts to organise the cargo ship *Campbell*, which was in Cairnryan, to go to the assistance of the *Princess Victoria*. But the *Campbell* was unable to get beyond the mouth of Loch Ryan. Maxwell also recalled the telephone calls he made to put various hotels on standby to accommodate any survivors.

Herbert Terry, a senior surveyor for the Ministry of Transport, also gave evidence on the seventeenth day of proceedings. He gave a detailed analysis of the amount of water that would have to be on the car deck and in the forward lounge to affect the stability of the ship. Herbert Steel, the chief surveyor for the Ministry of Transport, was then called and in his evidence and cross-examination, which filled nearly two days, he stated that at no time during the period 1947–1952 did the Ministry of Transport learn of any mishap to the ship resulting from her design or of any alterations made to her. He was asked if the two previous occasions when the ship had taken a list to starboard, on taking water into the car deck, indicated an inherent fault. Steel replied that the two previous occasions were simply accidents.

On the twenty-first day of the Inquiry, Thomas Rolland, a chief surveyor for the southern district of England for Registro Italiano (the Italian equivalent of Lloyd's), gave evidence. He stated that, in his opinion, the *Princess Victoria* was unseaworthy from the beginning and that he would not have passed the plans of the ship because of the stern doors, the opening in her stern and the want of freeing arrangements (or scuppers) on her car deck. He added that the stern doors were not adequate to exclude water from the car deck as it could still come over the top

of the guillotine door. There were also no proper freeing arrangements to deal with any large quantities of water on the car deck – the scuppers were only adequate to free water that was used for washing down the car deck. Rolland felt that having water trapped on a ship was a very dangerous situation. With regard to the scuppers, he stated that, according to the statutory rules, the ship should have had between 33 and 34 square feet of freeing port area on the car deck. As it was, the scuppers were only be about one square foot on each side.

Sam Batte, the radio operator at Portpatrick Radio station, was then called to give evidence and, like his colleague William McGregor and Coastguard William Spreadborough, he was to face penetrating questioning from Counsel. It was put to him, by Mr Chambers QC, that at 12.54 the Portpatrick lifeboat reached its apex going north while the *Princess Victoria* was going south, the two getting further apart. Batte answered, "It would seem so." The questioning continued:

Q. And nobody doing anything?

A. Well it was not my province Sir.

The chairman interrupted by saying that he did not think it was right to say that nobody was doing anything. Mr Chambers continued by asking Batte:

Q. But nobody doing anything to alter the lifeboat?

A. We had no authority to give the lifeboat a course to steer.

Q. Why then did you send the 13.22 message?

A. That was purely a personnel opinion – it was not an authorised message.

There followed three further days of final submissions and closing speeches from all Counsel. On 7 May Mr Campbell and his assessors visited the Great Northern Railway (Ireland) yard at Grosvenor Road in Belfast to view the four lifeboats recovered from the *Princess Victoria*. The Inquiry finally closed on 9 May, after having sat for 25 days, with Mr Campbell announcing that he and his assessors would sit in private on 26 May and take a further four or five days to complete their report.

The final Report was published in a 30,000-word, 22-page document on 11 June 1953. The main findings were that the *Princess Victoria* was in an unseaworthy condition

Mr JH Campbell and his fellow assessors inspecting the lifeboats of the *Princess Victoria* at Grosvenor Road railway sidings in Belfast.                    *S Herron collection*

arising from two circumstances: firstly, the inadequacy of the stern doors, which yielded to the stress of the seas, thus permitting the influx of water into the car space; and secondly, the inadequacy of clearing arrangements for the water which accumulated on the freeboard deck causing an increasing list to the starboard, culminating in the ship capsizing and foundering.

In the Report, Mr Campbell and his assessors then set about answering the 48 questions set by the Minister of Transport, Mr Alan Lennox-Boyd. Of these questions, number 15 was critical, as it asked if the ship was seaworthy when she left Stranraer. The answer was that she was not, and this matter was further discussed in the Annex to the Report.

With regard to whether the ship had been overtaken by an exceptional sea, the Report stated that there was no evidence of this. The Report added that initially the starboard sections of the stern doors were slightly stove in and the supporting stanchions buckled. This damage to the doors was sufficient to prevent them being closed; ultimately the sea burst both doors almost completely open.

The Report sought to attribute blame. Question 47 of the 48 Ministry questions asked if the loss was caused by the default of the owners and managers, the master or any other person. The answer given by the Report was that the loss of the *Princess Victoria* was caused by the owners and managers in the following respects: (1) in that they failed to provide stern doors sufficiently strong to withstand the onslaught of the heavy seas which may be reasonably

expected to occur from time to time in the North Channel; (2) in that they failed to provide adequate freeing arrangements for seas which might enter the car space from any source; (3) in failing to take precautionary steps after the incident of November 1951; (4) in failing to comply with the provisions of Section 425 of the Merchant Shipping Act 1894, in so far as they did not report the incident mentioned in (3) above.

Finally, Mr Campbell and his assessors were asked to consider if, in their opinion, the loss of the ship was due to any wrongful act or default of the owners, managers, master or any other person. The Report stated unequivocally that the owners and managers were in default. The court was of the opinion that the "superintendence" of the ship left much to be desired. The Report also stated that there was a lack of wise management, based on the evidence of one of the managers. For example, there was no one in the whole organisation whose sole duty it was to be in charge of the structure of the ship; the managers considered frequent visits to the ship to be unnecessary and were content so long as no major incident was reported to them.

In conclusion, the Report stated that the builders and Lloyd's Register of shipping should be absolved of any responsibility for the loss of the ship. This recommendation was due, the court stated, to the fact that neither the ship's builders nor the classification authority had ever been made aware of the previous incidents that had occurred on the vessel.

The court then placed on record the outstanding and selfless conduct of David Broadfoot, the radio officer on the *Princess Victoria*, who had stayed at his post to the last. Appreciation was also expressed by the court to James Kelly, master of the *Pass of Drumochter*, and to Hugh Nelson and the crew of the Donaghadee lifeboat. The Report stated that had the *Princess Victoria* been as staunch as the men who manned her, then all would have been well and this disaster averted.

There was, however, one dissenting voice. Professor AM Robb, one of the assessors, added a three-page addendum, dated 23 June 1953, to the main Report in which he stated in relation to the question who was at fault, "A contributory cause was default on the part of the compliment of the ship."

# The appeal

On 22 June 1953, at Westminster, the Minister of Transport, Mr Alan Lennox-Boyd, informed the House of Commons that following the loss of the *Princess Victoria* and the subsequent publication of the Inquiry into her loss, the Railway Executive had been in consultation with him. Mr Lennox-Boyd stated that steps had been taken to strengthen the stern doors in four comparable vessels, while arrangements had been made to increase the size of the scuppers on these ships.

Captain Orr, the Unionist Member for South Down, asked the Minister if it was possible to have a full debate on the loss of the *Princess Victoria*. The Minister replied that the Transport Commission had a period of 28 days in which to decide if they wished to appeal the decision of the Inquiry and that it would not be possible to discuss the matter until the Commission had decided what they intended to do.

On 7 July 1953 the British Transport Commission, the owners of the ship, announced their intention to lodge an appeal by issuing a statement which concluded: "As a result, the Commission are appealing against the findings contained in the report. Captain J.D. Reed, the registered manager of the ship is also appealing."

Section 66 of the Merchant Shipping Act of 1908 gave the owners the same right of appeal that previously was available only to the master of a vessel. It was decided that the Appeal would be heard in the Northern Ireland High Court and that the Lord Chief Justice for Northern Ireland, Lord MacDermott, would preside. He was to be assisted by Lennard C Burrill, Professor of Naval Architecture at Durham University, Captain Phineas S Robinson, a retired master mariner, and Mr John Wallace, a retired chief marine engineer. The first day of the hearing was set for Tuesday, 29 September 1953.

Mr CA Nicholson QC, who had previously represented the owners and Captain Reed at the main Inquiry, was to appear for the owners at the appeal, with Mr FA Reid appearing for Captain Reed.

Mr Nicholson informed the Lord Chief Justice that the British Transport Commission contended that the report from the Inquiry was "inconsistent, erroneous and unsatisfactory" and that there were four areas under which the appeal was being made. These were, he stated:

That the report should have found that the loss of the ship was caused by an exceptional sea condition, which could not have been reasonably foreseen.

That the report wrongly found against the owners and managers in respect of the design of the ship and its alleged unsuitability for the Larne–Stranraer route. The report should have found that the owners had reasonable grounds for believing that the ship was suitable for the route at all times.

The report was wrong in that it found that incidents in 1949 and 1951 established fault which caused or contributed to the disaster, by making the ship unseaworthy.

The findings of the court were against the evidence and were ambiguous, unjust, unsatisfactory and bad in law.

Mr Reid, on behalf of Captain Reed, lodged 13 grounds of appeal. In his opening address to the Lord Chief Justice, the Queen's Counsel argued that something quite unusual happened on 31 January: the ship had been sailing into the wind and was hit from the rear. He cited one witness at the Inquiry who said that he could not believe that this would happen. Reid said that if it was established that conditions on the day were so unusual, then no one could have expected it or foreseen that it would be the cause of such a disaster. This court, he argued, had to be satisfied that the sea conditions on that morning in January were such that no reasonable person could have made an error of judgement in failing to foresee it. Reid concluded by saying that it seemed extraordinary that the owners of the ship were found guilty and yet Lloyd's Register of Shipping, the builders William Denny, and the Ministry of Transport were all exonerated.

Throughout the next days of the appeal, the time in court was taken up with reading the evidence from the

Inquiry. At one stage Lord MacDermott informed the court that he was reading the evidence at home in order reduce the time in court.

At one point during the hearing an application was made to have Captain Perry, the previous manager of the ship, admitted into court. Lord MacDermott ruled against this request, stating that it was now too late for Perry to approach the court. He felt that Perry's main reason for the application was to try to seize an opportunity to lodge an appeal himself. The Lord Chief Justice added that Perry had had the opportunity to appeal, but had not taken this course of action at the time.

Over the ensuing days, counsel built upon their arguments. It was pointed out that Captain Reed was aware of one previous occasion when the stern doors had been forced in by a collision and not by the actions of the sea.

Mr Nicholson informed the court that the designs of the *Princess Victoria* numbers 1 and 2 had caused no concern, both ships giving good service to their owners. It was only after the disaster that witnesses came forward to give evidence on the allegedly poor design of the current *Princess Victoria*.

Mr Reid outlined to the Lord Chief Justice and his assessors the duties undertaken by Captain Reed. He informed the court that there was no marine superintendent based at Stranraer and that Reed operated from the headquarters in London. Reid stated that Captain Reed took over control of the *Princess Victoria* from Captain Perry and at that time no mention was made of any particular problems with the ship. He said that Reed was not a marine architect and therefore could not be responsible for any defects that the builders or owners of the ship had failed to see. Reid also informed the court that no charges or criticism had been brought against the previous manager, Captain Perry. He stated to the court that if the original findings were allowed to stand, the public may feel that the *Princess Victoria* should not have sailed on that morning and that Captain Reed may be left open to some form of public retribution. Mr McSparran QC, appearing for three trade unions, agreed that Captain Reed was not fully aware of the problems associated with the stern doors and that it was only after the loss of the ship that he managed to find out about the earlier incidents.

The appeal finally concluded on 13 October 1953. Lord MacDermott informed the court that he and his assessors would reserve their judgement and that the court would announce their decision at a later date. That judgement was duly delivered at the High Court in Belfast on Thursday, 26 November 1953. In a 13,500-word statement, which took 90 minutes to deliver, the Lord Chief Justice dismissed the appeal of the British Transport Commission, the owners of the *Princess Victoria*. He did, however, uphold the appeal of Captain Reed.

In his findings, the Lord Chief Justice stated that the owners were negligent on two counts: by not taking appropriate steps to ensure that water could be drained from the car deck; and for failing to make the stern doors strong enough to withstand the heavy seas from flooding the deck.

The court was also critical of the previous manager, Captain Perry.

Following the judgement, Captain Reed stated, " I am very glad indeed about my appeal being allowed, and this is a very great relief to me."

Just over a year after the loss of the *Princess Victoria*,

Lord Brookeborough, the Prime Minister of Northern Ireland in 1953. *PRONI*

Lord Brookeborough, the Prime Minister of Northern Ireland, received a letter from Lord Hugh Rathcavan in London, the one-time 'Father of the House of Commons' and the first Speaker of the Northern Ireland Parliament (he was also the uncle of future Prime Minister of Northern Ireland Terence O'Neill). The communication, dated 17 September 1954, had been requested by Brookeborough to determine if there should be a debate about the *Princess Victoria* disaster in the Northern Ireland Parliament. The writer pointed out to the Prime Minister, whom he referred to as "My dear Basil", that a manager with British Railways, Mr Malcolm Speir, had stated that when it was decided to alter the *Princess Victoria* to allow for the extra weight of the milk tankers, the ship's builders, William Denny, had said that the structure of the ship would be altered and an element of danger introduced. Rathcavan added that, in spite of these reservations, alterations were made and Speir was quoted as saying, "I felt the ship was never the same from that time onwards."

For some strange and unknown reason, Mr Speir was never called to give evidence at either the Inquiry or the subsequent appeal. This raises the question of whether the Inquiry did not want to hear this evidence, which would have dammed the builders for undertaking the work; or the owners for insisting that it was carried out; or possibly even the Ministry of Transport or Lloyd's Register of Shipping who passed the final work.

The original Inquiry was ordered by the Ministry of Transport. This Inquiry was to investigate all aspects leading up to the disaster, including the roles played by British Railways, the ship's builders, William Denny, the Ministry of Transport, and Lloyd's Register of Shipping. It would have been highly embarrassing to have produced a report which dammed the Ministry of Transport, while condemnation of the builders would have shaken confidence in British shipbuilding. The same would have applied had Lloyd's Register been found culpable. The 'safest' outcome was to let the owners suffer the blame for the loss of the *Princess Victoria*.

# The life jackets that killed

At the Inquiry several witnesses had suggested that many of the bodies they had seen in the water looked as if they had been choked by their life jackets. These witnesses felt that when the life jackets had contacted the water, they were pushed up the body of the wearers against their necks. The Report did suggest that alterations be made in the instructions for donning and wearing the jackets, but many people felt that the standard life jackets had actually killed more than they saved.

The life jackets carried on the *Princess Victoria* were standard cork life jackets, supplied by Steadman and McAllister of Glasgow. None of them had been replaced during the previous three years and it is possible that the 1,566 jackets carried were those originally supplied for the vessel in 1947.

An artist's impression of the standard cork life jacket.

*Barry Craig*

The specifications for a standard cork life jacket, as issued by the Board of Trade in 1946, stated that it would suitable for an adult or child, made of good quality cleaned cork, weighing not more than 12 pounds per cubic foot and capable of supporting 16½ pounds of iron in fresh water for a period of 24 hours. The outer material of the jacket was made of linen and had two pockets at the front and two at the rear. Two eight-foot-long tapes were provided to be tied around the middle of the wearer. The finished item was 30 inches long and 22 inches wide, weighing not more than four pounds and four ounces. The Board of Trade regulations also advised on the fitting of the life jacket: to be placed over the head and the tapes to be crossed at the front, tied in a half knot and then pulled tight before fully completing the knot.

On the subject of life jackets, David Brewster, the captain of the trawler MV *Eastcoates*, had remarked in a statement to the authorities prior to the Inquiry:

> We eventually got on board 7 persons in all, 6 who were dead, (the bodies were very stiff) 2 of the dead were in uniform and possibly crew, there was four women in all and one dead was a naval rating and 1 alive who was Petty Officer Beer and was semi-conscious. Those that were dead [had] their life jackets hard up under their chins giving me the impression that they had choked as they jumped overboard.

Brewster was called to give evidence to the Inquiry on 26 March. During in his evidence, Mr Topping, QC for the Ministry of Transport, asked if those he saw in the water were wearing life jackets. Brewster replied:

> Quite a lot of them were, and a lot of them had been choked in jumping into the water. I understand that quite a lot of people had to jump off the ship. I am sure that if anybody jumped from any distance at all into the water, these things would have come up and choked them straight away . . . The survivor that we picked up [John Beer] was semi-conscious when we got him aboard. Before we got him he was pulling his lifebelt down from his neck. He must have known that if he had let the lifebelt go, he would have choked.

Later that same day, Charles Thompson, a steward who had survived, gave his evidence with regard to the life jackets. He stated that the crew had been told to inform passengers of the possibility of injury when jumping into the water if they did not hold onto their life jackets. Mr Lowry, who also represented the Ministry of Transport, asked Thompson, "What were you told the danger was if that precaution was not taken." Thompson replied, "You might get your neck broken, or something else."

Further evidence regarding the life jackets and their affect on those in the water is found in the written statement of James Gilmore. He said that when he was on a raft he encountered many bodies floating in the water. Passengers had jumped in with life jackets on, and on impact with the water the heavy jackets had seemed to knock them out.

Denis Peck, in his written deposition, made mention of the attitude of the crew when handing out life jackets. He recalled that some of them just threw the life jackets into the lounge for the passengers and told them to get on deck. From this statement it appears that, at least for some passengers, there was little or no instruction given on how to don or subsequently use the life jackets.

In his deposition, Gilbert Kelly, a senior surveyor with the Ministry of Transport, made reference to the construction of the life jackets. Kapok life jackets, he said, were more comfortable than cork, Kapok being a softer material. At the Inquiry, Kelly was asked if jumping from a height into the water wearing a cork life jacket would result in the breaking of the neck of the wearer. He replied, "I cannot say, it may do."

A report, compiled by Captain J Taylor, was prepared to assist Mr Campbell and his assessors at the Inquiry. In this document, Captain Taylor quoted from Ministry of Transport Notice No M320, dated August 1948, which on page 14, paragraph 20, sub paragraph (iii) states:

> Impressing on passengers the risk of injury from jumping overboard and the importance of using the side ladders provided for the purpose of entering the boats should it prove necessary to embark in them after they have been lowered into the water.

Taylor further stated:

> There is no doubt that there is considerable danger in jumping into the water from a height to persons wearing either the Standard Cork life jacket or the Standard Kapok life jacket if they are not efficiently fitted because when the body hits the water a loosely fastened life jacket may be forced sharply upwards under the chin.

In 1923 the Board of Trade had made inquiries into the use of life jackets and the risk of injury being caused to the wearer when jumping into water from a height. This report came to the conclusion that life jackets should not be approved unless the buoyancy was so distributed that there would be no likelihood of injury if the wearer had to jump from a height. It was shown at the same time that this danger could not be wholly avoided, if the life jacket was to keep an inert body in a reasonably safe position in the water and so avoid the danger of the head of an unconscious person falling face forward into the water. This latter consideration was deemed the prime one in terms of preserving life. The problem of falling from a height was judged an acceptable risk, especially as persons on board ship would be expected to be lowered into the water in lifeboats. Only in extreme circumstances would they be expected to have to use the ship's ladders or jump into the water.

But this was not the case with the *Princess Victoria*. Those on board were standing on a ship that had turned over; those that could not hold onto the rails were flung into the water. Even those who managed to scramble over the rails were then faced with the prospect of having to jump into the water. The list in the ship ruled out the possibility of using the vessel's ladders to enter the lifeboats.

A few years ago, as part of my work with the Northern Ireland Fire Brigade, I attended a ship fire fighting course at the Fire Service College in England. Part of this course covered sea survival and to gain my certificate, I had to make a jump into open water and swim for a raft. I was kitted out in the latest design of survival suit, complete with a pre-inflated life jacket. The jump into the water was from a height of about five or six metres. Prior to the jump, the instructors went to great lengths to explain that I should cross my arms over the life jacket and pinch my nose, so that when I hit the water the life jacket would still be flat to my chest and no water would get up my nose.

Prior to the jump, I was reasonably calm. Even though the jump was not from a great height, when I entered the water, the grip of my arms relaxed and the life jacket was pushed slightly upwards, towards my face.

Imagine the situation on the *Princess Victoria* on 31 January 1953. Those people holding onto the side rails had been enduring the most horrific conditions for around six hours. For them, unlike myself, there would have been a confusion of emotions before jumping: fear, panic and the imminence of death in the freezing waters of the Irish Sea. For those who were flung off the ship as their grip on the rails was lost, there would have been little or no time to think about crossing their arms over the life jackets, even if they had been informed of this, before they hit the water below. Those that managed to hold on were then faced with the terrible and daunting task of having to climb over the rails and move along the overturned hull. When the hull turned bottom up, anyone not holding on would also have been flung into the water and quite possibly their reflexes would not have been quick enough to grasp the life jacket.

Captain Taylor's report concluded:

It is a practice, during an inspection of the life jackets at a boat drill, to emphasise the point that a loosely fitted jacket might be fatal to the wearer and in all probability break the neck if he found it necessary to jump into the water from a height. Again, during the drills Surveyors offer the advice that should the wearer have to jump into the water from a height he should place his hand at the collar opening in front and exert a downward pressure to counteract the upward pressure exerted by the buoyant medium of the jacket.

This advice may not have been given to the passengers on the ship. One of the recommendations of the Court of Inquiry was that the instructions for the wearing of cork jackets should be amended to include a reference to the need for holding them down in order to prevent the choking of the wearer. If that recommendation had been applied perhaps more people could have survived the loss of the *Princess Victoria*.

# Compensation

The front page of the *Belfast Telegraph* printed on Sunday, 1 February 1953. This was only the second occasion in the history of the 'Tele' that a Sunday edition was printed.

*Author's collection*

On Sunday, 1 February, just a few hours after the loss of the *Princess Victoria*, the *Belfast Telegraph*, for only the second time in its then 83-year history, published a four-page special Sunday edition of the newspaper. Hundreds of people gathered outside newsagents and the York Street offices of the newspaper, eager to find out any news on the fate of those on board the ship. The shocking news they read was that finally, after all night searching, only 44 men had survived the ordeal.

Such was the disbelief that this ship could have been lost on such a short sea crossing that, on the following day, Monday, 2 February, it was announced in the local press that a fund was to be set up to assist the dependents of those lost.

The Princess Victoria Distress Fund, as it was called, was jointly opened in the two ports between which the ship plied. In Larne, custody of the fund was entrusted to Sir Hugh O'Neill DL and the Mayor of Larne, Alderman Charles Ross MBE; while in Stranraer the Earl of Stair, the Lord Lieutenant of Wigtownshire and the Provost of Stranraer, Mr William Dyer, were nominated as sponsors. Within an hour of the opening of the fund, more than £400 had been raised. Lord Hurcomb, chairman of the British Transport Commission, sent a telegram to inform the sponsors that the Commission was to donate £1,000 to the fund.

The Fund was overwhelmed by donations from many local businesses and the general public, both locally and from far afield. Throughout Northern Ireland and south-west Scotland, local people organised fund-raising events with film shows, concerts, beetle drives, rowing and sailing events and general 'whip rounds' to collect for those who had been affected by the sinking of the ship. In the week following the loss, all the Belfast cinemas donated their profits to the fund and, along with collections from their patrons, raised almost £4,000. Many firms donated to the fund, Reid and Adams of Stranraer giving £100, the British Aluminium Company and their staff giving over £550. Donations also came from individuals as well, ranging from ten shillings (50p) given by a lady in Edinburgh, to a few pennies from young children's pocket money. From far-off shores the Johannesburg Irish Association sent a cheque for £100, while an anonymous donation from a 'regular passenger' of £100 was also received.

The committee of the fund decided that it should be closed on 3 May 1953 so as to work in conjunction with the Mayor of London's National Flood and Tempest Disaster Fund. This decision would allow the sponsors of the fund to apply to the government to match the donations from the general public; the Lord Mayor of London's National Fund eventually donated a further £103,189.71 to the monies raised by the public. By December 1953 the total raised by the fund had grown to over £180,000.

When the new fund was finally established in 1956, it was given the official title of 'The Lord Mayor of London's Princess Victoria Disaster Relief Fund'. At that time there were 64 widows, 85 children, 26 orphans and other dependents being assisted by the fund. Payments to the children were to cease when the child reached the age of 21, at which time the fund would make a lump sum payment to the person concerned.

At the time, payments, generally of £10 per week, were made to widows of those lost on the ship. They were given the opportunity of accepting a weekly payment or a one-off payment of around £3,000. Children were also granted financial assistance on a weekly basis. When the child reached 21 years of age, the fund made a final payment to them of around £125. Today there are still a few people receiving support from the fund.

The question of claims for personal injuries or loss was finally resolved when the British Transport Commission, which owned the *Princess Victoria*, finally agreed with the ruling of Lord MacDermott on their appeal against the findings of the Court of Inquiry. On 1 December 1954, the Commission issued a statement in London which declared that they would pay proper damages as may be agreed. The full statement read:

> The British Transport Commission have carefully considered the judgement delivered by the Lord Chief Justice of Northern Ireland on their appeal against the findings of the court of inquiry into the tragic loss of the M.V. *Princess Victoria* on January 31, 1953.
>
> While the appeal decision does not determine the liability of the Commission to pay damages in respect of those who perished or were injured in the disaster, the Commission do not propose, in view of the findings of the Lord Chief Justice, to dispute this liability or to seek to limit it under the Merchant Shipping Act, 1894.

The Commission are, therefore, prepared to pay to the persons entitled such proper damages as may be agreed. If agreement cannot be reached in any case, the amount of the damages will have to be determined by the appropriate court.

The statement then gave details of the address of their office, at which claims should be submitted, and ended with the following: "The Commission are studying carefully the various other matters raised in the judgement."

In their statement, the British Transport Commission also pointed out that they would not seek to limit their liability under the Merchant Shipping Act, 1894. This Act allowed the owners of vessels that were wrecked or lost to make an application to the Admiralty Court to limit the amount of compensation to £15 per ton of the ship's tonnage. In the case of the *Princess Victoria*, this would have meant the total liability would have been capped at £41,000, resulting in the relatives of those lost receiving only £300 each. As we shall see, some relatives received far in excess of this amount, while some only received the basic figure.

Six weeks later, on 12 January 1954, the first claim for compensation was heard at the Northern Ireland High Court. The claim by Mrs Martha Reid, whose husband Adam Reid was lost on the ship, was heard before Mr Justice Shell. The court was informed that Adam Reid had worked for Short Brothers and Harland at the Wig Bay factory and that his earnings were between £13 and £14 per week. It was directed that Mrs Reid be awarded the sum of £4,500 for the loss of her husband. Mr Justice Shell further directed that out of the main award, £1,660 should be set aside for their 12-year-old daughter.

By now, over 75 writs had been being issued against the British Transport Commission, the majority of them eventually being listed for hearing at the High Court. Relatives, including four small children, were using two Acts of Parliament in their claim: the Fatal Accident Acts (1846–1908), which allowed a claim to proceed for the loss and damage sustained by reason of the death caused by the negligence and breach of the statutory duty of the Railway Executive; and secondly, the Law Reform (Miscellaneous Provisions) Act (Northern Ireland), for loss or damage sustained to the estate of the deceased.

Some writs were issued by the wives of those whose who were lost, whilst some were issued by parents and executors of the estates of the deceased. The Invisible Mending Centre Ltd issued a writ in respect of loss and damage caused to them by the loss of the ship. The Inglis Bakery in Belfast also sought compensation for the loss of their two directors, the Piggot brothers. Some survivors lodged a claim for personal injuries, loss and damage.

By 10 February all of the writs had been heard and dealt with and compensation was paid at the following rates: for the loss of a husband, £4,500; for the loss of a son, £1,200; for the loss of a daughter, £1,200; for the loss of a wife, £750; and for the loss of a child, £300.

When deciding on the level of award to be paid for a wife that had been lost, the court decided that if she was not a wage earner, the husband could only claim a sum representing the value of her services to him. This type of ruling would obviously not be applied today.

A controversial award was made to the family of Billy Hooper, the 17-year-old pantry boy who worked on the ship. Even though he was old enough to work on board, the court decided that because he was under 21 years of age, he would be treated as a child and his family paid the lower sum of £300. His mother spent practically all of the award on a headstone for his grave in Larne Cemetery.

Thomas Peoples, the father of John Peoples, the mess room steward, lodged a civil claim against the ship's owners. Initially John's father was awarded £50 for the loss of his son from the Distress Fund. A year after the loss of the ship, Mr Peoples was offered the sum of £850 compensation from the British Transport Commission. In a letter to Mr Peoples' solicitor, the Commission argued that as John Peoples was so young there was every possibility that he may have married in the next few years and this was reflected in the offer made. Mr Peoples was not prepared to accept this, writing to the Commission to argue that what may have happened in the future, had his son survived, should have no bearing on the claim for his loss. A final offer of £950 was made by the Commission a month later, which Mr Peoples accepted.

Where the court made an award to a child, in some cases payment was deferred until the child reached the age of 21 years. However, the payments that were held in trust for the child did not keep pace with inflation or even reflect the accrued interest over the intervening years. In the case of one family, it was agreed that the son, aged five years of age in 1953, would receive £650 when he was 21; his sister, aged eight years, was awarded a lump sum of £450, again to be paid on her attaining the age of 21 years. When these two children reached the appointed age, the boy, after a 16-year wait, was awarded the sum of £650, while his sister received £312 1s 11d, representing a reduction of £137 18s 1d on the amount awarded 13 years previously.

However, one child did not receive compensation. The widow of William McClenaghan was pregnant and subsequently gave birth to a baby boy, who was named after his father. No compensation was provided for the upbringing of this infant.

Several of those who survived the sinking were paid small sums for their personal injury and loss. Albert Dickie lost all of his army kit when the ship sank. He approached a solicitor to see if he could claim for the loss, but was told that compensation would only be paid for personal loss. Some people from his local village held a collection for him and raised the sum of £39. He spent the rest of his army service paying off the lost kit.

Another soldier, George Wilson, also lost his kit; like Albert Dickie, he had been travelling in uniform. On his return to his regiment in Germany, he was also billed for the lost equipment. However, Wilson was approached by an officer from Ireland who told him that he would sort the matter out. The officer was true to his word and George heard no more about the matter.

The people on board the ship who survived were paid little or no compensation for the trauma or stress that they had suffered. George Wilson was told by his solicitor that claims would only be accepted by the court for injury or

Letter to Mr T Peoples, father of John Peoples, making a final offer of compensation for the loss of his son. *B Crawford collection*

loss. Today those people who were expected to 'just give themselves a shake and get on with life' would have been properly compensated for the terrible ordeal they suffered. One survivor whom I interviewed summed up attitudes in 1953 when he said that the words 'trauma' and 'counselling' had not been invented; perhaps he should also have included the word 'compassion'. There are not many survivors alive today, but many of those that are, still harbour nightmares about what happened all those years ago. Is it now too late to give them some form of compensation for the suffering they have endured in silence down the years?

# The search for the Princess Victoria

In 1973, 20 years after the *Princess Victoria* was lost, the memory of that terrible day had been long forgotten, except for those whose lives had been personally touched by the ship's demise. It was therefore no surprise that the announcement that the wreck had been located did not make headline news. The Royal Navy had been undertaking routine sonar mapping of the Irish Sea and had discovered a large object, five miles north-north-east of the Copeland Islands. The general feeling of anyone who took an interest in this news was that this was most probably the car ferry the *Princess Victoria*. The fact that the ship did not carry any special cargo or contents meant that the wreck was destined to be left in peace. There was no economic reason for an attempted dive to the vessel, especially as she was resting at a depth of around 52 fathoms of water and in an area where there were very strong underlying currents.

The wreck of the ship was to lie forgotten for another 19 years, until the directors of the British Broadcasting Corporation in Belfast decided that the Corporation was to become more actively involved in the production of new 'home-made' documentary series. In April 1992 they appointed Bruce Batten to head up a new factual team called the Topical Unit. The brief for this unit was to produce homespun factual programmes about Northern Ireland. Batten was given a clean sheet with the introduction of this new unit, naming the series *Home Truths*.

Linda McAuley, a broadcaster with the BBC, heard about Batten's new programme and knew that he would be on the lookout for stories. She informed him about the upcoming fortieth anniversary of the loss of the *Princess Victoria*. Also working at that time in the Ormeau Avenue studios was the daughter-in-law of survivor Billy Baird. A keen diver was also working in the new BBC unit and he suggested the possibility of diving down to the wreck. These people were the driving force behind the idea that the first *Home Truths* should feature the loss of the ship.

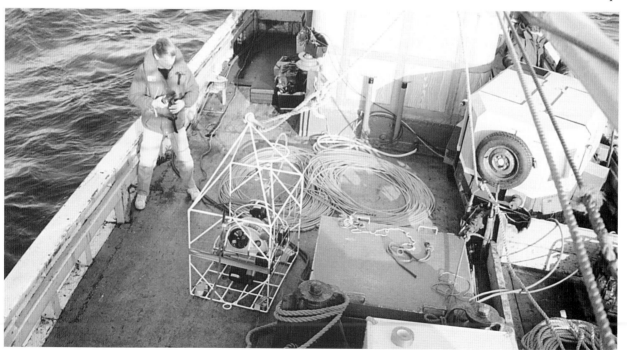

Preparing to send the camera below to search for the wreck of the *Princess Victoria*.    *All photos J MacKenzie Collection*

John MacKenzie, who led the Cromarty Firth Diving Services team.

**Left:** The deck of the search vessel is a hive of activity.

Many months were spent searching for survivors or anyone who would have a story to tell about that day back in 1953.

While research and production for the programme pushed forward, it was decided that as part of the transmission, the BBC would explore the possibility of commissioning a dive to the wreck. Batten contacted Cromarty Firth Diving Services, a Scottish company which specialised in diving using underwater sonar equipment and ROV (remotely operated vehicles), to help locate and then film the wreck of the ship.

In the middle of September 1992 a film crew from the BBC, led by Bruce Batten, accompanied John MacKenzie and the crew of Cromarty Firth Diving. They set sail from Bangor harbour in County Down on board a local fishing vessel, setting a course for the location of the wreck discovered by the Royal Navy some 19 years earlier. With the assistance of depth-finding and echo location equipment, they dropped anchor above the site of the wreck. The divers released an underwater Hyball ROV with camera, which was controlled through an umbilical line, using feedback from the camera to navigate to the wreck. From the control room in the fishing vessel, the crew of Cromarty Firth Diving were able to descend to the wreck using the anchor chain of the fishing boat as a guide downwards to the bed of the Irish Sea. Without too many problems, they came upon the wreck of a vessel lying on

The camera that would film the wreck on the seabed.

The monitor on board relays a picture of what is probably one of the *Princess Victoria*'s windows.

its port side and started to photograph what lay in front of them. This ship was very heavily covered in soft sponges that had attached to the hull but, undeterred, filming continued. After about 40 minutes, while sitting on the hull of the ship, the umbilical cord of the camera caught up on the wreck and snapped. As the only thing in contact between the camera on the seabed and the fishing boat on the surface was the umbilical cord, the camera was lost and the dive had to be aborted. However, there was some exciting news when the underwater footage was reviewed and the diving experts were able to identify two bilge keels and a support, which would have held a wooden rubbing strip as well as a scupper on the side of the hull. From this initial footage it looked as if the vessel may well be the *Princess Victoria*. But with the catastrophe of loosing the camera, nothing further could be done except raise the anchor and head back to Bangor.

On the journey back to the harbour, Bruce Batten, on viewing the footage taken, decided that a further dive would have to be made to the wreck and Cromarty Firth Diving set about having the camera replaced.

If this first tentative view of a ship lying on the seabed was actually the *Princess Victoria*, it would dispel rumours that the ship lay off the coast of Liverpool. In 1987 a Bulletin of Notice of Wrecks had been issued, stating that a wreck was situated in 100 feet of water, 16 miles from Liverpool. Four years later, in 1991, divers identified this wreck as the *Princess Victoria*. By request, this information was kept secret but it did start speculation that this was indeed, the ill-fated Larne to Stranraer car ferry. In fact it was another ship called *Princess Victoria*, a paddle steamer that had been built in 1889 and which had been sunk by a German U-boat in World War One.

Could the ship that Bruce Batten and the diving team discovered be the *Princess Victoria* which had sank in January 1953? There was now going to be an enforced wait while a replacement underwater camera was ordered and delivered to Bangor.

Exactly four weeks later, the members of the Cromarty Firth Diving Services team, along with the film and production crew from the BBC, met up again at Bangor harbour and set sail with a new underwater camera. On the surface, they quickly found the site of the ship, but in those four weeks the tides off the Copeland Islands had become faster, the sea was choppy and when the camera reached the seabed, MacKenzie found that visibility was extremely poor.

For two days, and after a total of four dives, the *Princess Victoria* was not to be found. The budget that was set for the dive was fast running out. There was only time for one further dive before the expedition would have to be called off. Practically at the last minute of the fifth dive, the television screen in the control room on the fishing boat showed the image of the hull of a ship. The images from the seabed were recorded as the camera made its way over the hull; this time the crew were able to identify the starboard cargo car deck door on the hull. They took the camera up to the promenade deck and were able to photograph the ship's railings and a porthole. After about 20 minutes of filming, the tide was running so quickly that navigating the camera became increasingly difficult and the final dive now had to be aborted.

When the camera was safely back on the fishing boat, the crew were able to closely study the recorded footage. After comparing the underwater film with the ship's plans, all were satisfied that 41 years on, they had indeed found the *Princess Victoria*.

With the ship now located, there was a marked grave for all those who perished all those years ago. The crew held a simple ceremony on the deck of the fishing boat and placed a wreath on the water in memory of those who had died in the cold waters of the Irish Sea.

# *The last fateful voyage* 16

The MV *Princess Victoria*

*Larne Times*

Should the *Princess Victoria* have perished with the terrible loss of life all those years ago? The answer in hindsight, is quite simply, no. The weather on that January morning was so severe that several ships had to seek shelter in Belfast Lough. Many other small vessels were in distress off the Scottish coast, north of Stranraer. The storm, or as many remember it, the 'Great Storm', was to see the North Channel exposed to force 12 conditions, yet the captain ordered his ship to sea. Today, shipping regulations, for example on the Stena HSS *Voyager*, clearly state that the vessel is only permitted to go to sea when conditions are no worse than a force 9 gale.

However, it was not just a question of weather on that occasion. In 1953 when the *Princess Victoria* foundered, there had been at least four previous incidents involving the ship. Two of these incidents, which involved water entering the car deck in large quantities, were never fully reported. There were also two collisions involving the ship, one of which occurred only a few months prior to her last fateful voyage, and also the modifications made to the ship in May 1949, which her builders were not happy about. Probably the most important factor in the loss of the ship was the major design flaw in the way the stern doors were arranged, in that they did not provide a watertight seal for the car deck. This problem was exacerbated by the attitude of her designers and builders who discounted the possibility that the vessel would ever be in a position where she would ship major quantities of water onto her car deck. Worse still was the fact that only a few weeks after the loss of the *Princess Victoria*, another ferry, the *Lord Warden*, also built by William Denny, nearly suffered the same fate in the English Channel, when she shipped a heavy sea over her closed stern doors onto the car deck. Yet nothing had been done to indicate to her captain or crew that there was a major problem with the 'open stern' design that had been employed in both these ships.

The four past incidents should have sounded a very clear warning to those responsible for the ship: the captain, her designated manager and her owners, British Railways. They should have seen how vulnerable the ship was. The open stern section and the folding half doors at the stern left the vessel and the car deck exposed in very bad weather. As any sailor 'worth his salt' knows, to have a large quantity of water or fluid moving about on an large enclosed deck is an extremely dangerous position to be in. Yet when this happened not once, but twice, nothing appears to have been done about it. What was more concerning was the apparent lack of communication between the captain and his designated manager, Captain Reed. Furthermore, officials from the Ministry of Transport and Lloyd's Register of Shipping appear either not to have known of these incidents or to have chosen to ignore them. This failure of communication was to ultimately lead to the loss of over 134 lives.

Captain James Dudley Reed had been appointed as the British Railways regional manager for Irish Shipping in January 1952. This position made him the designated manager of 25 ships, including the *Princess Victoria*. He had a staff of 11 assistant managers. His predecessor had been Captain Harry Perry, who had held the position from 1 January 1948.

Perry was to oversee several alterations to the ship. Captain Ferguson approached him with a concern that on occasion heavy spray was coming over the top of the stern doors and wetting the cargo. Perry contacted the ship's builders and it was decided that a sliding door be fitted over the top of the stern doors. This would extend the height at the rear doors by four feet and this work was carried out in May 1949. At the same time the car deck was strengthened to allow the ship to carry milk tankers at the after end of the ship. In 1951 Perry also received a complaint that there appeared to be buckling at a bulkhead in the engine room and up into the lower lounge. This was checked: some of the linoleum floor covering in the lounge was lifted where it had cracked, but the plates underneath were found to be satisfactory.

Perry should have been more aware of the consequences arising from these complaints about his ships. When told

of the 10 degree list that the ship had taken when the milk tankers overturned, he did nothing about the stability problem except approach the Ministry of Food to see if a better design of tanker could be made. He seemed to be confusing cause and effect.

After the incident in which the ship took a heavy sea on trying to enter Larne, resulting in water coming onto the car deck, Second Officer Unsworth later stated that he informed the ships' surveyor, Mr AL Finlayson. The conversation between the two men took place when the *Princess Victoria* was in dock during a subsequent routine survey. Finlayson later recalled the conversation with Unsworth, but his view was that while it would be a "considerable asset to have additional freeing arrangements made", he simply reported the matter to his head office. Finlayson stated that he did not "consider that the access of such water was a danger to the integrity of the ship". Finlayson's attitude, as a ships' surveyor, in some ways sums up the general view of many of those who had a responsibility for the design and use of the vessel.

However, the most blatant disregard for the ship's safety was shown by the chief draughtsman, Mr Elmer Cotton, of the ship's builders, William Denny, when he told the Court of Inquiry that it was never anticipated that a heavy sea would come over the top of the ship's stern doors. Cotton informed the court that when designing the ship the freeboard, or the height of the car deck above the water line, was 11 feet 6 inches. The rear gates at the open stern were almost five feet high, giving a combined height of almost 17 feet and he had never envisaged the ship being hit by a wave of that height. Possibly he should, at the designing stage, have contemplated what would happen if the ship was ever confronted with seas of that height or bigger.

With regard to the scuppers that were provided on the car deck to free trapped water, Cotton stated that they were not designed to clear large amounts of water, but were placed to allow for the removal of water used for washing down the car deck.

The total area of the car deck on the *Princess Victoria* was 6,503 square feet and the scuppers had a total area of 89.94 square inches. On a similar ship, the *Lord Warden*, the car deck was 14,900 square feet, while her scuppers had a total area of 230 square inches.

Mr Thomas Rolland, a naval architect and ship surveyor, stated in his evidence to the Inquiry that according to shipbuilding rules the scuppers on the *Princess Victoria* should have been between 33 and 34 square feet in area, but the scuppers that were fitted were about 1 square foot on each side of the ship.

The other problem with the ship's design was the fact that the rear of the vessel was only protected from the open seas by the stern doors. The complete stern of the ship was in fact open at the level of the car deck and the only thing keeping out the elements and the sea were the 4 foot 6 inch-high metal stern doors. Their main purpose was to stop things falling out of the ship, not stop the sea getting in. A person of average height could have stood on the car deck, looked over the doors and seen the sea. The design as employed meant that the car deck of the *Princess Victoria* was not sealed shut from the elements. This area was the Achilles heel of the vessel, in many ways a disaster waiting to happen.

As stated previously, Mr Campbell, the chairman of the Inquiry, had already raised the issue of the Larne incident, when the sea had come over the doors, pointing to the possibility of disaster in the future. Sadly, those responsible for the ship never took seriously the threat of water entering the open car deck.

An open space, such as existed on the *Princess Victoria*, would not be allowed on roll on/roll off vessels today. Designers now recognise the potential for disaster if the car deck on these ships is allowed to fill with water, with what is called the 'free surface effect' making the vessel unstable. This occurred, with terrible consequences, in 1987 when the *Herald of Free Enterprise* left harbour at Zeebrugge with her bow doors open and overturned within seconds. Further stark evidence of how free surface effect could have disastrous consequences was provided by the loss of the *Estonia* in 1994. Her bow visor was ripped way in a storm in the Gulf of Finland, resulting in water entering her car deck. Within 40 minutes she was lost. The sinking of these two ships resulted in 948 people dying.

A week after the loss of the *Princess Victoria*, *The Spectator*, in the column 'A Spectator's Notebook', featured an article on the loss of the ship. The author of the column signed himself or herself as 'Janus'. In the article, Janus asked two questions:

Should the captain have put back when the ship got beyond the shelter of land and encountered the full force of the gale? And was the construction of the ship, with folding doors in the stern to facilitate the loading of cars, always a potential danger?

The answer Janus provided to the second question may quite possibly dispose of the first.

The writer argued that the prime cause of the disaster was a defect in the structure of the *Princess Victoria*:

> . . . for doors are obviously less likely to withstand abnormal seas than a solid hull – then the captain was clearly helpless. Once the doors had been smashed in and the car-deck inundated, the ship, driven lower into the water by the weight of water she had taken in, was less and less able to resist the waves which continually broke over her . . . I write with complete ignorance of such matters, but that at any rate is how one aspect of the dreadful affair strikes a landsman.

The captain of any ship has the sole responsibility for the crew, passengers, cargo and safety of the vessel. His decision as to whether or not his ship sets sail is final. On land, he has the back-up of his manager and ship owners. On board, he has the assistance of his officers and crew, but he has the ultimate position of responsibility, and before commencing any voyage he should satisfy himself that his vessel is actually seaworthy. Thomas Rolland, the ship surveyor, stated at the Inquiry that in his opinion the *Princess Victoria* was not seaworthy because of the design of the stern doors and the freeing arrangements. Captain Ferguson must have at some time questioned the design himself. On one occasion, only five months before the loss, he told Captain William Morrow, one of the assistant managers under Captain Reed, that it might be useful to have additional scuppers on the car deck. Morrow later stated that the main reason for this request was the captain's expressed concern for the passengers getting their feet wet when they made their way to their cars, prior to disembarking. With no camber or slope on the car deck, any gathered water was not freely draining away. Morrow later stated that it took him seven months to finally discover why Captain Ferguson wanted the extra scuppers and felt that the request was related to the previous occasions when water had entered the car deck.

When Captain Ferguson decided to set sail on 31 January 1953 he was well aware of the weather forecast and the effects it would have on his ship crossing the North Channel. However, when he did find himself in great difficulty, with the ship overwhelmed by the full fury of the 'great storm', he was to prove that he was a very determined, courageous and capable officer, who would fight with all his might to save the *Princess Victoria* and those on board.

Once the storm was encountered, Ferguson and his ship were in an precarious position. If he had tried to push further northwards, the vessel would have encountered the full fury of the waves and quickly have been overwhelmed; if he had dropped his anchor to lie hove to, the shallow draught and high decks of the vessel would have left them at the mercy of the pounding waves. It was also impossible for the *Princess Victoria* to reverse into Loch Ryan, as the bow rudder could not be engaged This reversing manoeuvre would have resulted in more water being shipped into the car deck, as the ship backed into the loch.

There was only one course of action left open to Captain Ferguson and he made the very bold decision to try and 'run' to Northern Ireland. For the *Princess Victoria* to have continued to sit at the mouth of Loch Ryan would have meant certain death for all on board. He was to nurse the ship for a further 25 miles across the Irish Sea with her having at times a list of over 50 degrees, enough to test any captain. In the end, she got tantalisingly close to the safety of land.

Ferguson's decision to sail from Stranraer that morning may have been more that an a simple error of judgement on his behalf. There were reports in the newspaper that a few weeks previously he had refused to sail because of very bad weather, and was ordered to do so by the management of British Railways. Captain Reed, at a press conference two days after the loss of he ship, went to great pains to deny this account, stating, "I can assure you that he [Captain Ferguson] was never reprimanded." Reed also stated that it required a great deal of courage for the master of a ship to decide not to sail at the stipulated time.

The main reason for ensuring that the ship sailed on time was that the *Princess Victoria* carried the Royal Mail and that train timetables on both sides of the Irish Sea were set around the sailing times. It would have been inconceivable in the early 1950s that the ship would be delayed in crossing, with the knock-on effect this would have on both the railway operators and the Royal Mail. The unexpected presence on board of Maynard Sinclair, the Deputy Prime Minister of Northern Ireland, and Sir Walter Smiles MP was a further reason for the vessel not to be delayed. These two VIPs had already had their travel arrangements changed due to the weather and perhaps Captain Ferguson did not want to cause further delay.

After the loss of the ship, British Railways went to great lengths to dispel the rumour that they had ordered the *Princess Victoria* to sail, stating that there had never been an occasion when a manager had counter-ordered a ship to sea. The only source which might settle this matter – the ship's log book – lies at the bottom of the Irish Sea.

On 31 January 1953, the actions of Captain James Millar Ferguson and his crew in trying to save the ship and those on board, were beyond question. Ferguson, his crew and the passengers on the *Princess Victoria* were in the end let down by the design of the vessel and the sometimes blatant disregard for proper supervision by the owners, British Railways, and their managers.

In his Report into the loss of the *Princess Victoria*, the chairman, Mr JH Campbell QC, stated: "If the *"Princess Victoria"* had been as staunch as the men who manned her then all would have been well and this disaster averted." The disaster did occur, but it was a disaster that could have been avoided.

A basic rule of seamanship dictates that to go to sea, you must have a watertight ship. The wind, waves and weather will always find any weak spot on the vessel. The design of the MV *Princess Victoria*, with her revolutionary open car deck, meant that this simple rule could not be maintained.

In reality the loss of 134 lives in the afternoon of the 31 January 1953, and the subsequent pain and suffering that was caused to so many families amounted to death by design.

The Donaghadee lifeboat *Sir Samuel Kelly* restored to its former glory, situated in Donaghadee.　　　*Authors collection*

# *Appendix 1*

## *Princess Victoria* chronology

| | |
|---|---|
| 8 February 1945 | Initial inquiry placed by the London, Midland and Scottish Railway (LMS) with William Denny shipbuilders of Dumbarton. Subsequently an order for the new *Princess Victoria* was placed. |
| 27 August 1946 | *Princess Victoria* launched. |
| 28 February 1946 | *Princess Victoria* handed over to her owners. |
| 8 March 1947 | *Princess Victoria* delivered to Stranraer and entered service. |
| 1 January 1948 | Ownership of the *Princess Victoria* passed from the LMS to the British Transport Commission (British Railways). |
| May 1949 | A guillotine or sliding door is added to lock over the stern doors to prevent sea spray entering the car deck. The car deck is also strengthened to accommodate the carriage of milk tankers. |
| 25 November 1949 | En route to Stranraer, during heavy weather, two milk tankers overturned on the car deck. Their valves were opened and approximately 6,000 gallons of milk flooded the car deck. It took over 40 minutes to clear the deck of the spillage. |
| 20 September 1950 | While berthing at Stranraer harbour, the ship struck the quayside ramp, causing minor damage to her stern. |
| 25 November 1951 | While attempting to enter Larne in adverse weather conditions, the ship was hit by a heavy sea. Around 27,000 gallons of sea water entered the car deck. The stern doors were damaged by the water. The ship returned to Stranraer. It took 90 minutes to clear the water from the car deck. |
| 2 November 1952 | When tied up at Larne harbour, the ship was struck by the SS *Empire Gaelic*. The *Princess Victoria* was pushed backwards into the quay and damage was caused to the guillotine door at the stern. |
| 31 January 1953 07.45 | The *Princess Victoria* sets sail from Stranraer bound for Larne. |
| 08.50 | The ship leaves Loch Ryan and enters the Irish Sea. |
| 09.00 approx | The ship is hit by a wave, resulting in the stern doors on the car deck being laid open to the sea. |

| 09.15 approx | An unsuccessful attempt is made by several crew members, under the direction of the chief officer, to try to close the stern doors. The attempt was abandoned after about 15 minutes. |
|---|---|
| 09.30 approx | An unsuccessful attempt is made to release the bow rudder of the ship in an attempt to try to navigate back into Loch Ryan. |
| 09.46 | The ship transmits a XXX message requesting assistance at the mouth of Loch Ryan. There is a list of 15 degrees in the vessel. |
| 10.00 | HM Coastguard at Portpatrick contact Corsewall Point Lighthouse for news of any sighting of the vessel. |
| 10.22 | HM Coastguard request assistance from the Royal Navy. The tug *Salveda* is en route to offer assistance. |
| 10.30 | The list in the ship is so bad that the sea was clearly visible out of the starboard windows. |
| 10.32 | The *Princess Victoria* broadcasts the first SOS message giving her position as four miles north-west of Corsewall Point. |
| 11.00 | The Portpatrick lifeboat, the *Jeanie Speirs*, is launched to assist the *Princess Victoria*. The passengers are informed for the first time that the ship was passing through a difficult time. At Portpatrick Radio station an attempt is made using direction finding equipment to ascertain the true position of the ship. Only one bearing is recorded of 316 degrees. No action is taken on this information. |
| 11.10 | The *Princess Victoria* transmits a second private radio message to British Railways informing the ship's owners of her current position. |
| 11.26 | HMS *Contest*, a naval destroyer, sets sail from Rothesay bound for Corsewall Point in response to a call for assistance. |
| 11.35 | The list on the ship is estimated at 45 degrees. A third distress message is transmitted from the *Princess Victoria*, giving her position as five miles west-north-west of Corsewall Point. |
| 11.43 | HMS *Contest* informs the *Princess Victoria* by radio that her ETA will be 13.00. |
| 12.00 | The list in the ship is now 35 degrees. The weather is force 9 to 12. *Princess Victoria* transmits a series of letter Vs in an attempt to let other radio stations locate her. Direction-finding equipment is again employed. |
| 12.17 | Two bearings, from Malin Head and Portpatrick, show that the *Princess Victoria* is 12 miles to the north-north-east of Mew Island, off the coast of County Down. |
| 12.19 | The *Princess Victoria* transmits a radio message stating her position as 280 degrees from Killantringan, near Portpatrick. |

| 12.20 | Approximately 500 tons or 112,000 gallons of water is on the car deck of the ship. |
| 12.52 | The *Princess Victoria* transmits that her starboard engine room is flooded and her position is critical. |
| 13.00 | The list in the ship is now around 60 degrees. The passengers are informed that HMS *Contest* will be with them at about 13.15 |
| 13.08 | The engine room is flooded and the ship's engines fail. The *Princess Victoria* transmits a SOS message stating that the ship is stopped and on her beam ends. |
| 13.15 | The *Princess Victoria* transmits that they are preparing to abandon ship. |
| 13.25 | The *Pass of Drumochter*, an oil tanker anchored in Belfast Lough, overhears radio transmissions and proceeds to go to the aid of the *Princess Victoria*. |
| 13.30 | The passengers are told to assemble on the weather deck and be prepared to abandon ship. |
| 13.35 | The *Princess Victoria* transmits that she can see the Irish coast. |
| 13.40 | The Donaghadee lifeboat, the *Sir Samuel Kelly*, launches to the assistance of the *Princess Victoria*. |
| 13.58 | The *Princess Victoria* makes her last radio transmission, stating that she is five miles east of the Copeland Islands. |
| 14.00 | The *Princess Victoria* turns over completely and then sinks. The *Orchy* and *Eastcoates*, anchored in Belfast Lough, proceed to assist the *Princess Victoria*. |
| 14.49 | The *Orchy* informs Portpatrick Radio that they are among people on rafts. |
| 15.00 | The *Pass of Drumochter* takes a lifeboat in tow to protect it from the waves. The Donaghadee lifeboat rescues those people in the lifeboat. |
| 15.30 | HMS *Contest* rescues six men in a lifeboat. The Portpatrick lifeboat, the *Jeanie Speirs*, rescues two men on rafts. |
| 18.00 | The *Sir Samuel Kelly* docks at Donaghadee harbour with 33 survivors. |
| 19.15 | The *Jeanie Speirs* docks at Donaghadee with two survivors. |
| 21.30 | The *Sir Samuel Kelly* returns to sea to continue the search for survivors or bodies. |
| 22.00 | HMS *Contest* docks in Belfast harbour with eight survivors. |

1 February

| | |
|---|---|
| 01.30 | The *Sir Samuel Kelly* docks at Donaghadee harbour after a rendezvous in Belfast Lough to transfer passenger John Beer and several bodies from the *Eastcoates*. |
| 05.00 | HMS *Contest* and HMS *Woodbridge Haven* commence a search for bodies. |
| 07.00 | The *Sir Samuel Kelly* commences a search for bodies. |
| 19.15 | The *Sir Samuel Kelly* returns to Donaghadee with bodies. |
| 19.30 | HMS *Contest* and HMS *Woodbridge Haven* dock at Belfast harbour and offload recovered bodies. |
| 23 March 1953 | The Inquiry into the loss of the *Princess Victoria* commences at the Crumlin Road Courthouse in Belfast. |
| 11 June 1953 | The Final Report of the Inquiry is produced. |
| 29 September 1953 | An appeal against the findings of the Inquiry begins at the High Court in Belfast. The appeal is brought by the British Transport Commission and Captain Reed. |
| 26 November 1953 | The Lord Chief Justice of Northern Ireland delivers his ruling on the appeal. He dismisses the appeal of the British Transport Commission, but upholds that of Captain Reed. |
| 1 December 1953 | The British Transport Commission, the ship's owners, agree to pay damages in respect of the loss. |
| 12 January 1954 | The first claim for damages is heard at the High Court. For the loss of her husband, Mrs M Reid is awarded £4,500. |
| 10 February 1954 | All claims for loss have been settled at the High Court. Seventy-five claims were settled by the court, while six were settled out of court. |
| 8 July 1962 | A memorial to the *Princess Victoria* is unveiled and dedicated at Stranraer. |
| 1973 | The Royal Navy locate a shipwreck off the Copeland Islands near the last given position of the *Princess Victoria*. |
| September 1980 | A memorial to the *Princess Victoria* is unveiled at Larne. |
| September 1992 | The wreck of the *Princess Victoria* is located and filmed by the BBC. |
| 26 January 1993 | The quest to locate the ship is the subject of the BBC Northern Ireland television documentary *Home Truths*. |

# *Appendix 2*

## *Princess Victoria* crew  (bold type indicates survivor)

| Name | Address | Post |
|------|---------|------|
| Ball, Robert C | Windsor Road, Belfast | fifth engineer |
| Baxter, Roseann | Gardenmore Park, Larne | stewardess |
| **Blair, James** | **Salisbury Terrace, Larne** | **steward** |
| Blair, William C | Glynn View Avenue, Larne | steward |
| Borland J Charles | Belmont Road, Stranraer | chief steward |
| Brennan, Hugh | Crescent Gardens, Larne | purser |
| Broadfoot, David | Royal Avenue, Stranraer | radio operator |
| Campbell, John A | Liddesdale Road, Stranraer | able seaman |
| Clarke, Catherine | Arran Road, Gourock | bureau assistant |
| Close, Mary D | Bay Park, Larne | stewardess |
| **Craig, Alexander WB** | **West End Terrace, Stranraer** | **able seaman** |
| Duckels, Shirley | Bowling Green Road, Stranraer | chief officer |
| Ferguson, Captain James | Craigenelder, Stranraer | master |
| Freel, Edmond | Ashbrook Crescent, Belfast | fourth engineer |
| **Garrett, John** | **Stranraer** | **able seaman** |
| Gowan, William | Glencairn House, Portavogie | carpenter |
| Hardie, William | Broomfield Gardens, Stranraer | quartermaster |
| Hooper, William | Bank Road, Larne | pantry boy |
| Kerr, Wesley | Fleet Street, Larne | steward |
| Leckie, Fergie | Sun Street, Stranraer | quartermaster |
| Locke, Horace | Albert Street, Larne | pantry man |
| McAllister, Alex | John Simpson Drive, Stranraer | greaser |
| **McAllister, William** | **Gloucester Avenue, Larne** | **pantry boy** |
| McCarlie, William | Dalrymple Street, Stranraer | bosun |
| McCowan, James | Stranraer | second steward |
| McGarel, William | Glynn Road, Larne | quartermaster |
| McInnes, William | Fairhurst Avenue, Stranraer | third officer |
| **McKinnon, Malcolm** | **Castle Kennedy, Wigtownshire** | **able seaman** |
| **McKnight, John** | **Exchange Road, Larne** | **chief cook** |
| McMillan, David | John Simpson Drive, Stranraer | pantry man |
| **McQuiston, Thomas B** | **Mount Vernon Road, Stranraer** | **cargo man** |
| Mann, William | Coastguard Cottages, Larne | luggage man |
| Mayne, James | Curran Street, Larne | assistant steward |
| Morgan, Gerald | Beechwood Drive, Stranraer | second steward |
| Morrow, James A | Carnalbana, Ballymena | assistant purser |
| **Murdoch, John** | **Stranraer** | **able seaman** |
| Murray, Douglas | Glynn Road, Larne | greaser |
| **Nelson, Angus McKay** | **Oakland Avenue, Stranraer** | **able seaman** |
| O'Neill, Archibald | Glynn View Avenue, Larne | steward |
| Parker, William | Waterloo Road, Larne | second steward |
| Peoples, John | Mountjoy, Recreation Road, Larne | mess room steward |
| Porter, John | Royal Avenue, Stranraer | third engineer |
| Pritchard, Edward | Mountvernon Road, Stranraer | assistant cook |
| Rankin, James | Murrayfield Avenue, Stranraer | greaser |
| Ross, Allan | Church Street, Stranraer | second steward |
| Shields, Patrick | Sallagh Park Central, Larne | assistant steward |
| Taylor, John | Regent Park Grove, Morecambe | second engineer |
| Thomas, Albert J | Fairhurst Avenue, Stranraer | chief engineer |
| **Thompson, Charles E** | **St John's Street, Stranraer** | **second steward** |
| Wallace, John | Agnew Crescent, Stranraer | assistant steward |
| White, Leonard A | West point, Ballygally | second officer |

# *Appendix 3*

*Princess Victoria* passengers  (bold type indicates survivor)

| Name | Address |
| --- | --- |
| **Baillie, Mr Robert** | **Enfield Drive, Belfast** |
| **Baird, Mr Frederick WB** | **Elmer, Upper Greenisland** |
| **Baker, Mr Walter** | **Milne Road, Rochdale** |
| **Beer, Mr John V** | **Strathnairne Street, Cardiff** |
| Bilney, Lt Cdr AN | RAF Anthorn, Cumberland |
| Bilney, Mrs Rebecca HT | RAF Anthorn, Cumberland |
| **Bingley, Mr Geoffrey** | **Killmarsh Road, Hammersmith, London** |
| Bonnar, Mr Thompson | Mill Street, Larne |
| Borland, Mr William F | George's Street, Stranraer |
| Brown, Mr Samuel H | Antrim Road, Belfast |
| Bryson, Mrs Nancy A | Cremona, Castlerock |
| Carlin, Mrs Eileen G | St Ninian Place, Prestwick |
| **Carlin, Mr James M** | **St Ninian Place, Prestwick** |
| Carter, Mr William | Carncastle, Larne |
| Childs, Mrs Joyce | Wharf Road, Portsmouth |
| Childs, Mr Leslie | Wharf Road, Portsmouth |
| Childs, Master Stephen | Wharf Road, Portsmouth |
| Clarke, Mr Thomas | Owenstown, Ballysnod, Larne |
| Clarke, Mr George H | Cooperative Street, Derby |
| **Clements, Mr James** | **Coastguard Cottages, Larne** |
| Coleman, Mr Harry W | Finclair, Drains Bay, Larne |
| Connery, Miss Marie | Carrick Drive North, Glasgow |
| Connery, Mrs Mary | Carrick Drive North, Glasgow |
| Connolly, Mr Robert M | Mary Street, Newtownards |
| **Cooper, Mr Samuel** | **Sallagh Park Central, Larne** |
| **Copley, Mr William LT** | **Alliance Avenue, Belfast** |
| Craig, Mr Robert | Upper Waterloo Road, Larne |
| Crawford, Mrs Elizabeth | Galgorm Street, Ballymena |
| Curry, Mr James | Roden Street, Belfast |
| **Curry, Mr Thomas R** | **Donard Drive, Lisburn** |
| **Deans, Mr Robert** | **Mains, Stewarton** |
| **Dickie, Mr Albert** | **Ardreagh Terrace, Aghadowey** |
| Dingle WRNS, Miss Violet | Enfield, London |
| **Doak, Mr A** | **Belfast** |
| Driver, Mrs Catherine | Earlston Avenue, Glasgow |
| **Driver, Mr Patrick** | **Earlston Avenue, Glasgow** |
| Dummingan, Mr William | Newington Avenue, Larne |
| Fitzgerald Mr Edlin J | Oliver Plunkett Avenue, Dun Laoghaire |

| | |
|---|---|
| **Fitzpatrick, Mr John** | **Lowther Street, Workington** |
| **Flack, Mr Ernest FW** | **Laharna Avenue, Larne** |
| Francey, Mr David RJ | Feenanmore, Moneymore |
| Gault, Mr Thomas | Martinez Avenue, Belfast |
| Gillanders, Mr David S | Charaville, Dublin Road,Enniskillen |
| **Gilmore, Mr James** | **Crumlin Road, Belfast** |
| Gunn, Mrs Mary | Draperstown |
| Hamilton, Mr David W | Gortin, Carnlough |
| Hammond, Mr William A | Little Victoria Street, Belfast |
| Hanna, Mrs Jane | Troopers Lane, Carrickfergus |
| **Harpur, Mr Robert** | **Lough View, New Cumnock, Ayrshire** |
| **Harrison, Mr Kenneth B** | **Stackhouse, Settle, Skipton** |
| **Hastings, Mr Joseph** | **Bann Street, Belfast** |
| Heggarty, Mr Adam | Nissen Huts, Gloucester Avenue, Larne |
| Jackson MBE, Miss AVE | Eglantine Avenue, Belfast |
| Jewhurst, Major Frank G | Cherryhill Drive, Belfast |
| Johnston, Mrs Florence | Rushfield Avenue, Belfast |
| Kelly, Mr Robert | Wallasey Park, Belfast |
| **Kerr, Captain James** | **Kinvarra, Serpentine Road, Belfast** |
| Kipling, Mr Dudley F | Caw Villa, Limavady Road, Londonderry |
| Lowe, Mr James E | Flush Green, Belfast |
| Lowther, Mr Thomas J | Loopland Park, Belfast |
| **McAteer, Mr Donal** | **Thorburn Road, Belfast** |
| McCarter, Mr Dominic F | Walmer Street, Belfast |
| McClatchy, Mr | Belfast |
| **McClean, Mr Robert** | **Ballyness East, Bushmills** |
| McClenaghan, Mr William | Mealough, Carryduff |
| McCready, Mr Alexander | Hillmount, Islandmagee |
| McCready, Mr Alfred | Greyabbey Road, Ballywalter |
| McDonald, Mr Ian | Broomfield Gardens, Stranraer |
| McDowall, Miss Phillomena | Whitsun Avenue, Stranraer |
| McKay, Mr James A | North Approach Road, Belfast |
| McLaughlin, Mr Patrick J | St Crones Terrace, Dungloe, Donegal |
| McLaughlin, Mr R | Cullingtree Road, Belfast |
| McMurtry, Mr Andrew | Drummond Street, Larne |
| McNeill, Mrs Agnes M | Ava Drive, Belfast |
| McNeill, Mr Ronald G | Ava Drive, Belfast |
| McReynolds, Mr Samuel M | Rosebrook, Carrickfergus |
| Magee, Mrs Margaret | Drumraymond, Toomebridge |
| Magill, Mrs Helen | Belfast and Portpatrick |
| Magill, Mr John A | Belfast and Portpatrick |
| Mason, Mr Richard | Drumate House, Markethill |
| **Megarry, Mr David P** | **Millfort Avenue, Dunmurry** |
| Milligan, Mrs Isabella S | Tobermore Road, Magherafelt |
| Mitchell, Mr Victor B | Espie Way, Belfast |
| Mooney, Mrs Iris M | Knocktayde View, Ballycastle |
| Mooney, Master John | Knocktayde View, Ballycastle |

Mooney, Master Kevin — Knocktayde View, Ballycastle
Moore, Mr Hubert J — Richardson Street, Belfast
Moore, Mrs Martha — Richardson Street, Belfast
Moore, Master Victor — Richardson Street, Belfast
Morrow, James — Roddens Lane, Larne
Morton, Mr Thomas — Ainsworth Avenue, Belfast
Mullan, Mr Francis — Ballymully, Limavady
Mullan, Miss Rose Mary — Coolnasillagh, Garvagh
**Murray, Mr John G** — **Devonshire Street, Belfast**
O'Connor, Doctor Joseph — Gateshead, Northumberland
Parker, Mr William N — Ava Gardens, Belfast
Patterson, Mr Wolsey W — West Street, Carrickfergus
**Peck, Mr Denis** — **Saxmunden, Suffolk**
Petrie, Mr Alex — Loch Ryan Street, Stranraer
Piggot, Mr John S — Osbourne Gardens, Belfast
Piggott, Mr Lennox D — Osbourne Gardens, Belfast
Prentice, Miss Eileen S — Downe, Farnborough
Prior, Mrs Ada E — The Bay, Carnlough
Reid, Mr Adam M — Armitage Street, Belfast
Ritchie, Mr Robert JH — Newington Avenue, Larne
Robinson, Mr Ivan C — Neely Street, Belfast
Rosborough, Mr Robert J — Ogilvie Street, Belfast
**Ross, Mr John G** — **Loughmorne, Carrickfergus**
**Rotherham, Mr Kenneth T** — **Bishop Road, Liverpool**
Rowlands, Mr AP — Durranhill Road, Carlisle
Russell, Miss Lily — Kiltoy, Letterkenny
Shankland, Mr Gerald J — Hilltop Avenue, Cheshire
Sinclair MP, Major John M — Deramore Park South, Belfast
Smiles MP, Sir Walter D — Poratvoe, Donaghadee
**Stanford, Mr John R** — **Midland Road, Kettering**
**Sterling, Mr George W** — **Cavour Street, Belfast**
Sumner, Mr James — Clonmel, Tipperary
Sweeny, Mr — Republic of Ireland
Tatchel, Mr Albert — Dorset
**Thomas, Mr Ivor J** — **Wygan Place, Cardiff**
**Wallace, Mr James** — **Upper Woodburn, Carrickfergus**
White, Mr Robert — Stirling Avenue, Belfast
Willis, Mr Norman — Severn Street, Belfast
**Wilson, Mr George A** — **Hawkins Street, Londonderry**
Wilton, Mr John A — Enfield Street, Portstewart
Wordsworth, Mrs Geraldine — The Riding, Newcastle-upon-Tyne
**Yeomans, Mr John S** — **Prospect Road, Farnborough**

# *Appendix 4*

## Survivors' locations

**Rescued by HMS *Contest***

*From rafts:*

James Gilmore

John Murray

*From lifeboat No 2:*

Robert Baillie

Joseph Hastings

Donal McAteer

David Megarry

Kenneth Rotherham

Charles Thompson

**Rescued by MV *Eastcoates***

*From raft:*

John Beer

**Rescued by Portpatrick lifeboat**

*From rafts:*

William Copley

John Yeomans

**Rescued by Donaghadee lifeboat**

*From raft:*

John Fitzpatrick

*From lifeboat No 5:*

Malcolm McKinnon

*From lifeboat No 6:*

Frederick Baird

Walter Baker

Geoffrey Bingley

James Blair

James Carlin

James Clements

Samuel Cooper

Alexander Craig

Thomas Curry

Robert Deans

Albert Dickie

A Doak

Patrick Driver

Ernest Flack

John Garrett

Robert Harpur

Kenneth Harrison

James Kerr

William McAllister

Robert McClean

John McKnight

Thomas McQuiston

John Murdoch

Angus Nelson

Denis Peck

John Ross

John Stanford

George Sterling

Ivor Thomas

James Wallace

George Wilson

A fourth lifeboat was recovered several days after the loss, when it was washed ashore at Kearney Point in County Down. This boat contained the bodies of Edward Pritchard, Frank Mullan and Edmond Freel.

# *Appendix 5*

## Crew and passenger manifest

**Number of persons travelling on board**

|            | Male | Female | Children | Total |
|------------|------|--------|----------|-------|
| Crew       | 48   | 3      | 0        | 51    |
| Passengers | 98   | 25     | 4        | 127   |
| Total      | 146  | 28     | 4        | 178   |

**Number of survivors**

|            | Male | Female | Children | Total |
|------------|------|--------|----------|-------|
| Crew       | 10   | 0      | 0        | 10    |
| Passengers | 34   | 0      | 0        | 34    |
| Total      | 44   | 0      | 0        | 44    |

**Number of bodies recovered**

|            | Male | Female | Children | Total |
|------------|------|--------|----------|-------|
| Crew       | 31   | 1      | 0        | 32    |
| Passengers | 49   | 18     | 1        | 68    |
| Total      | 80   | 19     | 0        | 100   |

19% of the crew survived
26% of the passengers survived

The Final Report from the Inquiry incorrectly stated that there were 49 crew and a total of 127 passengers on the ship. In a radio message, transmitted at 11.57 hours, the *Princess Victoria* stated that she was carrying 60 crew and 123 passengers.

# *Appendix 6*

## Radio messages transmitted

08.06     *Princess Victoria* to GPK [Portpatrick Radio call sign]
"I am now leaving Stranraer bound Lame."

09.46     *Princess Victoria* to GPK-X.X.X. [urgency signal]
"Hove to off mouth of Loch Ryan. Vessel not under command. Urgent assistance of tug required."

10.31     Alarm signal re SOS. GMZN [*Princess Victoria's* call sign].

10.32     *Princess Victoria* to SOS.
"*Princess Victoria* four miles north-west of Corsewall. Car-deck flooded. Heavy list to starboard. Require immediate assistance. Ship not under command."

10.34     GPK to *Princess Victoria*
"R. SOS."

10.35     GPK to CQ [all ships]
Alarm signal.

10.43     GPK to *Princess Victoria*
The destroyer *Contest* proceeding from Rothesay to your assistance. Estimated time of arrival 14.00."

10.54     *Princess Victoria* to GPK
"SOS."

10.54     *Princess Victoria* to SOS.
"We require immediate assistance now."

11.00     *Princess Victoria* to SOS.
"*Princess Victoria* GMZN four miles north-west of Corsewall. Require immediate assistance."

11.14     GPK to *Princess Victoria*
I have a message for you. Portpatrick lifeboat launched to your assistance."

11.25     *Princess Victoria* to GPK
"SOS. Position approximately five miles WNW from Corsewall."

11.35     *Princess Victoria* to SOS.
"*Princess Victoria* GMZN. Position approximately five miles WNW from Corsewall. Car-deck flooded. Very heavy list to starboard. Ship not under command. Require immediate assistance."

11.43     Destroyer *Contest* to *Princess Victoria*
"Am proceeding to your assistance with all dispatch. ETA 13.00. Request details of extent of flooding and list. Have you power? If so, voltage a.c. or d.c.?"

11.57   *Princess Victoria* to *Contest*
"35 deg. list to starboard. Approximately 200 tons water and cargo in car-deck. Power 220 volts d.c.
123 passengers, 60 crew. Position approx. five miles W. by S. of Corsewall. Master GMZN."

12.11   *Princess Victoria* to *Contest*
"Have started radar. Will try to get bearing."

12.17   GPK to CQ
"SOS. Following received from British ship *Princess Victoria* at 10.34 GMT. Begins: SOS. Position five miles
W. by S. of Corsewall. Bearing from Portpatrick 282 deg. Bearing from Malin Head Radio 112.5 deg."

12.32   *Princess Victoria* to *Contest* and GPK
"Approx. position 280 deg., seven miles from Killantringan. Position grave but list not appreciably worsening."

12.43   *Contest* to *Princess Victoria*
"Regret will not reach you until 13.30. Are you in danger of sinking? If not, intend to pass tow on arrival and
proceed  to shelter of Loch Ryan for trying to send over a pump."

12.46   GPK to *Princess Victoria*
"What is your approx. distance off Scottish shore, ref. your radar?"

12.47   *Princess Victoria* to GPK
"Sorry, radar no use. Too much list."

12.52   *Princess Victoria* to GPK
"Position critical. Starboard engine-room flooded."

12.52   GPK to CQ
"SOS. Following received from British ship *Princess Victoria* at 12.52. Begins: SOS. Position critical.
Starboard engine-room flooded. Bearing from Portpatrick Radio 264 deg. Bearing from Seaforth Radio 312 deg."

13.07   *Princess Victoria* to *Contest*
"SOS."

13.08   *Princess Victoria* to CQ
"SOS. Now stopped. Ship on her beam end. Snap bearing 260-262."

13.15   *Princess Victoria* to GPK
"We are preparing to abandon ship."

13.21   *Princess Victoria* to *Contest*
"Can you see us?"

13.26   *Contest* to *Princess Victoria*
"Cannot see you yet."

13.30   *Contest* to *Princess Victoria*
"My ETA is now 14.15. Can you hold out until then?"

13.35   *Princess Victoria* to GPK
"SOS. Endeavouring to hold on but ship on beam end. Can see Irish coast. Shall fire rocket if you wish."

13.39   *Contest* to *Princess Victoria*
"Good luck. Am coming as fast as I can. Please fire a rocket."

13.47    *Princess Victoria* to SOS [GPK]
"Captain says he can see . . . lighthouse . . . off entrance Belfast Lough. Sorry for Morse."

13.47    GPK to *Princess Victoria*
"Is it Copeland?"

13.47    *Princess Victoria* to GPK
"Yes."

13.47    GPK to *Princess Victoria*
"Can you get a bearing?"

13.48    *Princess Victoria* to GPK
"Captain sez he can see Lighthouse . . . opeltnd [sic] . . . off entrance Belfast Lough. Sorry for Morse."

13.49    *Princess Victoria* to GPK
"Sorry, can't see it for squall."

13.54    *Princess Victoria* to GPK
"SOS. Estimated position now five miles east of Copelands, entrance to Belfast Lough."

13.54    *Princess Victoria* to GPK
"Sorry for Morse, OM [Old Man]. On beam end."

13.54    GPK to *Princess Victoria*
"R. Do not let that worry you, OM."

13.58    *Princess Victoria* to *Contest*
"SOS. Estimated position now five miles east of Copelands, entrance to Belfast Lough."

13.59    GPK to CQ
"Bearing *Princess Victoria* at 13.56, 250 deg. Class B (+ or - 5 deg.)."

14.31    *Pass of Drumochter* to MV *Lairdsmoor*
"Have you seen anything on your radar screen?"

14.32    *Lairdsmoor* to *Pass of Drumochter*
"Something on the screen; maybe it's him."

14.33    *Lairdsmoor* to *Pass of Drumochter*
"Something big east. Picked up ship on port bow."

14.35    Aircraft GAJNE to GPK
"Looking for *Princess Victoria*. Are you in touch with her?"

14.35    GPK to GAJNE
"Yes. Last known position was five miles east of Copelands, entrance Belfast Lough."

14.35    Portpatrick Radio to *Pass of Drumochter*
"Give me your position."

14.36    *Pass of Drumochter* to Portpatrick
"Checking my position. Can see something on port bow five miles."

14.36½   *Pass of Drumochter* to Portpatrick
"Copeland 2½ miles due south but ship we see is a destroyer."

14.37½   *Pass of Drumochter* to Portpatrick
"Ask *Princess Victoria* to fire rockets."

14.39    GPK to *Princess Victoria*
"Nil heard. Please, if possible, fire rockets, fire rockets."

14.42    *Orchy* to Portpatrick
"Have you any later position of *Princess Victoria*. Cannot see anything on radar."

14.45    Portpatrick to *Orchy*
"No news. What range are you using?"

14.46    *Orchy* to Portpatrick
"Three miles range."

14.49    *Orchy* to Portpatrick
"Have come across oil and wreckage and life jackets approximately five miles east of Mew Island.

14.50    *Orchy* to Portpatrick
"We see people on the rafts."

14.53    GPK to aircraft GAJNE
"Infs. coming in on R.T. Wreckage and oil in position five miles east of Copelands lighthouse."

14.53    *Orchy* to Portpatrick
"People on rafts waving."

         Portpatrick to *Orchy*
"Do your best."

14.54    Portpatrick to all ships
"All ships make for the position of *Orchy*."

14.55    *Pass of Drumochter* to Portpatrick
"We are one mile off *Orchy* and proceeding at full speed."

14.55½   *Pass of Drumochter* to Donaghadee lifeboat
"Now three miles north-east of Mew Island."

14.56    Donaghadee lifeboat to *Pass of Drumochter*
"Blow your horn to let destroyer know where you are."

14.58    *Orchy* to Donaghadee lifeboat
"Come to me. I am among people and bodies."

14.59    Portpatrick to *Orchy*
"Come on the air with your position."

15.01    *Orchy* to Portpatrick
"Five miles east of Copeland and drifting quickly."

15.03     *Orchy* to Drumochter
"There are a lot of people here but they cannot get hold of the line."

15.05     *Pass of Drumochter* to *Orchy*
"We are very low in the water, so we may be able to do something."

15.07     *Orchy* to Portpatrick
"Position hopeless. Cannot lower lifeboats but doing our best."

15.08     Portpatrick to *Orchy*
"O.K. Keep your chin up."

15.09     Portpatrick lifeboat to Portpatrick
"Ask big ships to guide us to position."

15.11     Donaghadee lifeboat to *Pass of Drumochter*
"Four miles east of Mew Island."

15.12     *Pass of Drumochter* to Portpatrick
"Coming up to lifeboat full of people."

15.13     *Lairdsmoor* to *Pass of Drumochter*
"Coming up to you with lines, etc."

15.14     *Orchy* to all ships
"All lifeboats please come to me."

15.15     *Pass of Drumochter* to *Orchy*
"We are coming up to two lifeboats."

15.15½    Portpatrick to *Pass of Drumochter*
"Can you give me your exact position?"

          *Pass of Drumochter* to Portpatrick and Donaghadee lifeboats
"We are 4½ miles north-east of Mew Island."

15.17     *Pass of Drumochter* to Donaghadee lifeboat
"If you see a ship with a black funnel and white bands go to her."

15.20     Portpatrick lifeboat to Portpatrick
"See three steamers; am going straight for them."

15.21     Portpatrick to Portpatrick lifeboat
"Some boats in vicinity fire rockets. If they cannot do that, start blowing whistles."

15.22     *Pass of Drumochter* to Portpatrick
"Two lifeboats, one with one in it and one nearly full."

15.23     *Pass of Drumochter* to all lifeboats
"If you can pick anyone up, you can put them on us, as our decks are low."

15.25     *Pass of Drumochter* to Portpatrick
"I am trying to get near lifeboats."

15.25½    *Orchy* to Donaghadee lifeboat
"Can you see us? Are you in the vicinity? Please come to us."

15.26    *Pass of Drumochter* to *Orchy*
"Have you got anyone?"

15.27    *Orchy* to *Pass of Drumochter*
"The position is hopeless. The ship will not do anything for us."

15.27½    *Pass of Drumochter* to *Orchy*
"We cannot get alongside lifeboat, but the chief is going to pour fuel oil over the side and we will do our best, as I have a brother-in-law there."

15.30    Portpatrick to trawler *Eastcoates*
"They are picking up survivors four miles north-east of Mew Island."

15.31    Unknown transmitter
"There is a hell of a sea. Can hear an aircraft overhead."

15.32    *Lairdsmoor* to Portpatrick
"In the vicinity of *Orchy* and wreckage, but no people."

15.34    Portpatrick to Portpatrick lifeboat
"How are you getting on?"

15.34½    Portpatrick lifeboat to Portpatrick
"Heading for tanker, but very heavy seas and cannot see very much."

15.38    *Orchy* to *Lairdsmoor*
"Are you getting me?"

15.39    *Lairdsmoor* to Donaghadee lifeboat
"There is wreckage here but no people."

15.39    *Orchy* to Donaghadee lifeboat
"There are people between me and *Lairdsmoor*. Can you come to us?"

15.40    *Orchy* to *Pass of Drumochter*
"Donaghadee lifeboat is coming to us now. He will be able to do better than we can, as our light ship is high and the position is hopeless."

15.45    *Lairdsmoor* to Portpatrick
"Position five miles north-east of Copeland but only see wreckage. See numerous rafts but no one on them."

15.47    Portpatrick lifeboat to Portpatrick
"See boats but no living people."

15.47½    Portpatrick to Portpatrick lifeboat
"Proceed to *Orchy*. There are lifeboats with people on them."

15.48    Portpatrick lifeboat to Portpatrick
"Proceeding with all speed."

15.51    Donaghadee lifeboat to *Pass of Drumochter*
"Come over to us, as we cannot do anything."

15.52    Donaghadee lifeboat to *Pass of Drumochter*
"We are coming to you."

15.53    *Orchy* to Donaghadee lifeboat
"Come over between us and the destroyer. There are people on raft."

15.54    *Orchy* to Portpatrick
"Can see the Portpatrick lifeboat."

15.56    *Pass of Drumochter* to *Orchy*
"The Donaghadee lifeboat is alongside one of the lifeboats and will transfer them to us."

15.59    *Pass of Drumochter* to Donaghadee lifeboat
"There is another lifeboat off us with one in it. We will go up to windward and make lee for you. Will you follow us?"

15.59½    Donaghadee lifeboat to *Pass of Drumochter*
"Yes, we will follow."

16.03    *Pass of Drumochter* to *Lairdsmoor*
"The Donaghadee lifeboat is picking up one boat and is taking the other man out of the other boat. We have poured oil out and it doesn't seem to be much good."

16.07    *Pass of Drumochter* to Donaghadee lifeboat
"The other boat is on our beam. We are making a lee for you. Come up close to us and if you wish to put them on board, you can."

16.09    Portpatrick lifeboat to *Pass of Drumochter*
"Can you direct me to any more people?"

16.10    *Pass of Drumochter* to Portpatrick lifeboat
"There is wreckage between me and the *Orchy* but I don't think there is anyone in it."

16.13    Donaghadee lifeboat to *Pass of Drumochter*
"Can you see any more people?"

16.14    *Pass of Drumochter* to Donaghadee lifeboat
"The *Orchy* says there is a lifeboat to windward of me. Can you see if there is anyone in it?"

16.18    Portpatrick lifeboat to all ships
"Can you direct me to anything?"

16.18½    *Orchy* to Portpatrick lifeboat
"Cannot see anything. Fear it is all over, but if we do see anything we will direct you."

16.23    *Lairdsmoor* to Portpatrick lifeboat
"There is a ship's lifeboat abeam of me now."

16.24    Donaghadee lifeboat to *Lairdsmoor*
"That is an empty lifeboat."

16.24½    *Lairdsmoor* to Donaghadee lifeboat
"There's a flashing light on the water. Don't know if it is a lifeboat or what it is."

16.30    Portpatrick to Donaghadee lifeboat
"How many survivors have you?"

16.30½    Donaghadee lifeboat to Portpatrick
"Cannot count them but should say about 40."

16.33    *Pass of Drumochter* to *Orchy*
"I am going through a lot of lifeboats but no sign of life."

16.34    *Orchy* to *Pass of Drumochter*
"No sign of life here, but we will cruise around for a little while longer. I am afraid nothing can last in this."

16.35    *Lairdsmoor* to *Pass of Drumochter*
"We can see nothing either. Nothing whatever can live in that."

16.36    *Pass of Drumochter* to Donaghadee lifeboat
"We cannot see anything only lifeboats and life jackets but will cruise around until dark."

16.37    *Pass of Drumochter* to Donaghadee lifeboat
"Can you find out if any more lifeboats were launched? It is funny that there were no women among the survivors."

16.40    *Lairdsmoor* to *Pass of Drumochter*
"I have cattle on board and they are getting great abuse, so at 17.00 we shall have to make for shelter so that they may be fed."

16.45    *Pass of Drumochter* to Portpatrick lifeboat Aircraft has dropped flares ahead of us, so we are going up to see what it is and we will direct you."

16.49    *Pass of Drumochter* to Donaghadee lifeboat
"If you can take them [survivors] into Donaghadee you had better do so, as it would be difficult to transfer them and something might happen."

16.51    *Pass of Drumochter* to Donaghadee lifeboat
"We have just passed through a lot of wreckage and lifeboats but no sign of life. I expect that is what the aircraft saw."

At 17.50 the *Pass of Drumochter* told Portpatrick that she had been through the wreckage again and had seen no sign of life, and at 17.34 *Orchy* radioed "Can do nothing more. Am going back to Belfast Lough."

There were two private messages sent from the *Princess Victoria* to her company:

1. 09.56 hrs. to Marine, Stranraer, Marine Office, Stranraer Harbour.
"Hove to, vessel not under command, have asked for immediate assistance of tug. Signed Ferguson."

2. 11.10 hrs.
"Have sent distress call; 4 miles North West Corsewall; car deck flooded; heavy list to starboard; require immediate assistance; ship not under command. Signed Ferguson."

There were no private messages sent in reply.

# *Appendix 7*

## Ship's specification

| | |
|---|---|
| Builders | William Denny & Brothers Ltd.<br>Dumbarton, Scotland |
| Shipyard number | 1399 |
| Gross tonnage | 2694.28 |
| Registered tonnage | 1405.28 |
| Date of construction | 1946 |
| Ships registry number | 168901 |
| Owners | London, Midland & Scottish Railway Company<br>The vessel was acquired by the British Transport Commission on 1 January 1948. |
| Port of registry | Stranraer |
| Plying limits of ship | "On voyages not exceeding 10 hours duration on Channel services in the Home Trade from Ports between Dover and Newhaven inclusive on the South Coast and between Holyhead and Oban inclusive on the West Coast." |

Passengers

First class
| | |
|---|---|
| On deck | 418 |
| In cabins main deck | 44 |
| In cabins boat deck | 12 |
| Main promenade and boat deck saloons | 510 |

Third class
| | |
|---|---|
| Promenade and boat decks | 382 |
| Promenade deck saloons | <u>149</u> |

|  | Total | 1515 |
|---|---|---|

| | |
|---|---|
| Designated crew number | 51 |
| Total passengers and crew compliment | 1566 |
| Life-saving apparatus | Lifeboats class 1 attached to davits 5 to hold 280 persons<br>Motor lifeboat class B attached to davits 1 to hold 53 persons.<br>30 buoyant seats each consisting of one upper unit for 20 persons and two lower units for 14 persons, giving a total spaces for 1440 persons. |
| | 12 lifebuoys |
| | 1566 cork life jackets (all certified May 1952) |

# *Appendix 8*

## Ship's plans

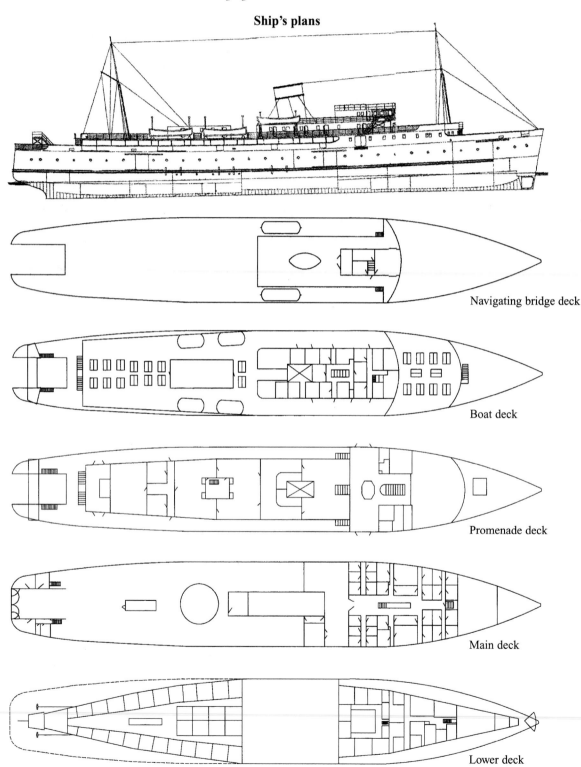

Navigating bridge deck

Boat deck

Promenade deck

Main deck

Lower deck

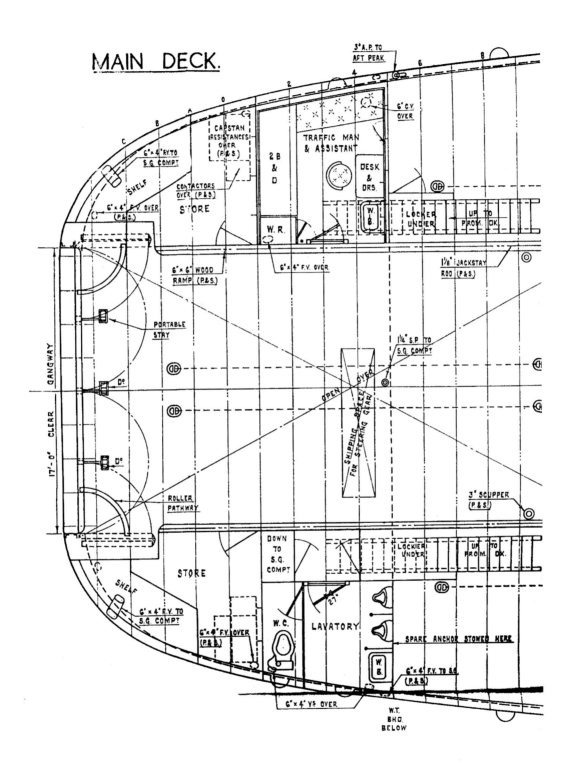

Plan view of the vulnerable stern doors on the car deck.

*PRONI*

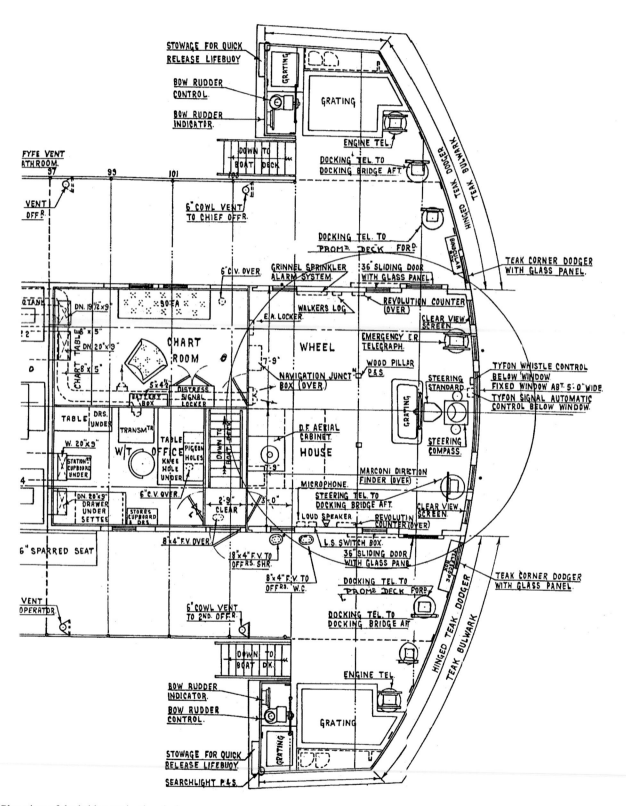

Plan view of the bridge navigating deck.

*PRONI*

# *Sources*

## Interviews

| | |
|---|---|
| Jack Adamson | August 2001 |
| Linda Armstrong | January 2002 |
| Jean Baxter | April 2001 |
| Lilly Brady | April 2001 |
| Hazel Campbell | December 2001 |
| Vicky Cloy | August 2001 |
| William Copley | March 2001 |
| Betty Crawford | February 2002 |
| Albert Dickie | January 2002 |
| James Gilmore | January 1993 |
| Agnew Hamilton | March 2001 |
| Sheena Herron | January 2002 |
| Nancy Johnston | August 2001 |
| Pat Leahey | January 2002 |
| Jim Locke | August 2001 |
| Diana Lockhart | January 2002 |
| Reverend Dr Lynas | March 2001 |
| Michael Lynch | March 2002 |
| Ian Macdonald | September 2001 |
| Reverend McAdoo | March 2001 |
| Jim McCarlie | April 2001 |
| Nat McClean | April 2001 |
| Ella McClenaghan | May 2001, September 2002 |
| Mr McKinley | March, May 2001 |
| John McKnight | August 2001, September 2002 |
| Captain R Mann | March 2002 |
| Ann Moore | March 2002 (including previously taped interview in 1992 with James Blair) |
| Hugh Nelson | November 2001 |
| Tommy Peoples | April 2001 |
| John Ritchie | May 2001 |
| Albert Steele | August 2001 |
| Janet Thompson | January 2002 |
| Margaret Thompson | May 2001 |
| John Wallace | August 2001 |
| June Waring | February 2002 |
| George A Wilson | February 2002 |

## Primary sources

Public Record Office of Northern Ireland:

    COM /64/4/58 – HM Government file on *Princess Victoria*

    D3830 – *Princess Victoria* documents

    D2506 – Report of Inquiry

    KB/19/689–691 – NI High Court Issue of Writs

Official Publications:

    Department of Transport, *Report of Court No 8074, MV Herald of Free Enterprise*, HMSO, 1987

    Department of Transport, *Report of Court No 7980, MV Princess Victoria*, HMSO, 1953

## Newspapers

*Belfast Telegraph*
*Belfast Newsletter*
*The Community Telegraph*
*County Down Spectator*
*Irish News*
*Irish Times*
*Larne Times*
*News Chronicle*
*Newtownards Chronicle*
*Northern Whig*
*Sunday Post*
*Wigtown Free Press*

## Periodicals

*John Bull Magazine* – Kerr, J Lennox, 'The Great Storm', 1954
*Past and Present* – Sanders, K and Hodgins, D, 'British Rail', No 19, 1995
*The Spectator*

**Books**

Brodie, Malcolm, Linfield, *100 Years*, Linfield Football and Athletic Club, 1985

— *The Tele: A History of the Belfast Telegraph*, Blackstaff Press, 1995

Cunningham, RR, *Portpatrick Through The Ages*, Portpatrick, 1985

Hunter Jack, *The loss of the Princess Victoria*, Stranraer & District Local History Trust, 1998

Kemp, P, ed, *The Oxford Companion to Ships and The Sea*, Granada Publishing, 1979

Kerr, J Lennox, *The Great Storm*, GG Harrap & Co Ltd., 1954

McCreary, Alf, *A Vintage Port*, Greystone Press, 2000

MacHaffie, Fraser G, *The Short Sea Route*, T Stephenson & Sons Ltd., 1975

McKillop, Felix, *Glencloy: A Local History*, Ulster Journals Ltd, 1996

Pollock, William, *Last Message 13.58: Death of the Princess Victoria*, Greystone Books Ltd, 1990

Wilson, Neil, *Great Sea Disasters*, Paragon, 1998


**Television and Radio**

BBC1, Northern Ireland; *Home Truths*, Producer / Director Bruce Batten, first broadcast 26 January 1993

Granada Television; *The Savage Planet*, Director Kate Coombs, first broadcast, 17 August 2000

# *Index*

Italics indicate a picture of or relating to the subject.